CU00922336

ONE OF A LEGION

ONE OF A LEGION

Cynthia C. Bell

The Book Guild Ltd
Sussex, England

The Book Guild Ltd
25 High Street,
Lewes, Sussex

First published 1995
© Cynthia C. Bell 1995

Set in Times

Typesetting by PPS Limited, Amesbury, Wiltshire

Printed in Great Britain by
Antony Rowe Ltd.
Chippenham, Wiltshire

A catalogue record for this book is
available from the British Library

ISBN 0 86332 965 9

Prologue

My first meeting with Norman was on one of his visits to see his sick father, who because of the seriousness of his condition, was allowed visits outside visiting hours. Each morning at 7.30 a.m. when I was on duty on the surgical ward, N would wait at the ward door for permission to enter. Evenings were just the same. This went on for very many weeks into months.

During one of his visits, whilst I sat writing up the day's report, N came up to the desk grinning and presented what he called two knitting needles he had found on his dad's bedside chair. The embarrassment I felt nearly choked me as I said thank you. He knew, as I did, that they were bougies, used for dilating the urethra of a prostate gland, and these had been forgotten during my off-duty.

Norman's visits continued in the same way: 'Good morning' and 'Good evening' went on and on. Eventually (presumably after taking stock of me) he asked if he could take me out. I stuttered and stammered, being taken by surprise. The difficulty was getting time off work, as lectures often took up our free time in the evenings. Our souls were not our own – you had to conform, like it or not. Time off could be switched without notice. Apart from one day off, we only had one evening free. However, we managed to clinch an evening and went to a nearby picture house along the street from my place of captivity.

Oh yes! In my mind I used to blame Florence Nightingale for the situation I was in, as I only knew her then for carrying a lamp around. Ours was a life of devotion and selflessness based on hers. She was well connected financially. Our wages were about £22 per year and we had no other means of support. It was a treat to go of a morning to Fowlers Cafe for a piece of sponge cake with pears and cream and a cup of coffee, costing about 1s (5p).

Nursing lectures had to be attended. These could happen even in off-duty time or day-off. Night duty was the worst. You could have lectures before going on duty at 7 p.m., then have one 'eck of a right pell-mell and another lecture at 10 a.m. Having a bath toned us up for the 10 a.m. and we had to force ourselves to do this. I must say there was always plenty of hot water and we knew it would save time when ready to go on again at night. If there was a lecture in the evening, then we had to toe the line again. It was no good complaining about fatigue – only if you had something septic or had spots. Once I did get some spots on my chest in earlier days and reported this to the night nurse who called us up at 7 a.m. for day duty. This was then reported to Night Sister who reported to Matron, who reported to the Home Sister. When the night nurse saw my spots, she said 'Oh they are only syphilis.' I knew I was a pure girl, but played up to this nurse, and if she got a laugh out of it, so did I! I thought it was rather a base remark, yet only meant in fun.

In 1937 I became a State Registered Nurse (SRN) with a 100 per cent pass in my finals and an Excellent Certificate on leaving. Being almost penniless, I joined a nursing agency for more lucrative work for about three years. I rented a flat – well, one room. N. was a first-class joiner.

My work took me away for weeks here and there and a bond had developed between us. One day, while leaning on a five-barred gate in the pouring rain, we decided to put our small change into a post office account, when and how we could. N had commitments at home, paying 25s (£1.25). board and 12s. (60p) rent and train pass daily into town to his place of work. His wages were something like £3 11s. 2d. (£3.56). We many times had to help each other out with coppers to get back home. He had an insurance to pay weekly at 1s. 6d. ($7\frac{1}{2}$p). I'm sure there would be work insurance stamps too.

My work took me away to Scampton. While I was there, I'm certain that one day the 'Dam Buster' planes passed over us. There was great tension and seriousness as we all stood in the garden watching these majestic and powerful creations of man going over. Even today, when ever I see a plane I say,

'God bless the pilot.' Eyes lifted up to the sky; one lady's knickers dropped and after a faint scuffle she rushed indoors.

N. and I, both having truly paid the cost for our training, felt worthy of our hire. One could get work in those days. It was a time also when hospitals were upheld by public subscriptions. About once a year there would be an Egg Sunday for the hospitals – a voluntary gift from all and sundry and put down in ISING GLASS for preservation and need.

N. continued in work in town until he was called up for training on 4 June 1942. By this time I had already been inducted into the Civil Nursing Reserve by the government. Every person fit and able was thrown into the war effort. My job was to prepare for theatre work and admissions. Huts had been built to accommodate and everything ready for need. They were mainly built and attached to Poor Law institutions on the outskirts of inland small towns.

N. and I wrote like billy-o during very long separations. He was still returning to his place of work in the evenings, doing ARP work later into the village he lived in. Having sorted out the care and consideration for his parents, (his mum was 65 years and his dad eighty years old), he was on his way for army training at Elgin in Scotland. At least he would get away from town, which was being regularly attacked by Jerry – 'Guns belching and firing like Hell in protection' (his words).

Sapper N Bell 2160917
'C' Company
No 6 TBRE
Pinefield Camp
Elgin Morayshire

4 June 1942

Elgin

I've arrived and first impressions are favourable. Left home by train into town at 6.40 p.m. but didn't arrive here until 3.00 a.m. It was actually quite a bit late. The train left our town at 7.30 p.m. arriving at York 9.15 p.m., so I went into town and found a pub which didn't turn out until 10.30 p.m. I got back to the station and we moved off at 11.30 p.m. The train was packed but I managed a corner seat. I only had a few winks of sleep. One couldn't stretch in any direction without kicking somebody else and it was terribly hot. We travelled on through the night and dawn started to break about 3.00 a.m., forming a lovely red sky and by 4.00 a.m. it was daylight. We ran along tight to the sea for miles by Dundee and Aberdeen, then changed and came inland, passing miles and miles of forests and lovely stretches of water and lochs with little islands studded about, which were smothered with rhododendron in full bloom.

At last we arrived here and were marched to camp by a lance-corporal who met us in. We were allotted our hut and bed, then off for kitbag, three blankets, shoes, tooth and cleaning brushes, basin, soap, comb and towel, knife, fork and spoon. Then we went for a dinner of balls of sausage meat, potato, cabbage and gravy, followed by a sweet. It tasted grand to my hungry stomach. After that we marched for interview and signing on, etc. The day being free, I was glad of a shower, spending quite some time between the hot and cold water. I'm off for tea now. Please write as soon as possible as I will.

Always yours, N.

Fortunately we had had a lovely weekend at my parents' home, which enabled us to have memories to live on. Lovely bracing walks with an outing on the moors – we were both fresh air fiends.

Elgin
5 June 1942

Here I am and to tell you how I'm managing. It is beautiful again, really hot and blue sky. I understand we can have showers every day, so that will be grand. I got a letter off to Mum and Dad. The majority of us have been to watch a football match in the camp until 8.00 p.m., then went off to the NAAFI. So, as there was no beer, I went for a lie down and lights went out at 10.15 p.m. until the bugle call. I got up, washed and shaved, made my bed 'just so' and swept the hut. The porridge for breakfast I ate with very little relish; then we were given a plate of kidneys each man. There are hundreds of men, so where do they get them all from? I've never tasted anything like the tea we drink morning and evening!

I've had to knock off and see the MO. All he did was to look in our mouths, under arms, our 'luggage' and hands. An orderly examined our vests and shirts, (for lice I presume), then it was off to the dentist who took a record. At ease until tea, when we have to parade. Now I'm off for a shower.

N. loved football and was a schoolboy international at eleven, playing for England against Scotland with two caps and three silver badges to his credit and honours on his school notice board. Mind you, I'd found out that he was no good at dancing! At this time, I was at another posting and I was left in the porter's lodge for over an hour until someone took notice of me when I first arrived there. It seemed these institutions didn't like our intrusion, as I was to discover in other moves. The porter was rather a brusque type and made attempts to know my pedigree. So having to wait with him for so long, I was fencing against his nosiness. He had a lad of fourteen as an assistant with jobs – a patient in the institution – I felt it quite deeply when I found he helped within the mortuary and raised the matter. It just didn't seem right for a lad of his age.

6 June 1942

At last I'm khaki all over except for boots – great tough heavy things. I have a little more kit yet to get – badges, second pair of boots and battledress. Now we are expected to act like soldiers. Haven't had much to do yet and went for a longed-for pint of beer. It had arrived in the NAAFI. Found plenty drinking. It looked awful and tasted worse, thick and muddy, smelling sour. One sip was enough, then I was on to the lemonade. After a bit of jaw I went to bed.

We are to have two half-days off a week – Thursday and Sundays – and we are to be 'let out' next Thursday. We really seem to be filling in time with gardening, cutting grass and doing the flower beds, which didn't have any flowers in. Have been told off by CQMS to get my hair cut. We are having a lot of short sharp showers and west winds – well I think they are westerly. Bacon and beans for breakfast, corned beef, cabbage and mash for dinner and rice pudding with raisins.

I expect that I'll hear from you tomorrow with all the news and reassure my aching heart. I don't suppose there will be any leave for at least four months. It would upset the sergeant major if I took a weekend off. Have yet to get my kit marked. The RE's Dance Band is playing for us tonight for two hours. Sort of to lighten our darkness.

I don't know anybody really as yet, although there's one from Hull, Patrington, Nafferton, Skipton, Huddersfield, Leeds and York, London, Lancashire, Derby and half a dozen Scots and a good few from Tyneside. In fact from all over England and Scotland. I've changed huts and I'm in No. 1 section with a Scot on either side. Expect I'll be talking a new language when I get home. Our battledress does stink. It must be the oily dressing. I'll have to make a list of what we have to cart around so that nobody pinches. Take care, N.

2160917 Sapper N Bell
Section 1
647 Party
'C' Company
No 6 TBRE
Pinefield Camp
Elgin Morayshire

10 June 1942

Some address what! Will use this from now on. Thanks for your letters. I intend writing you on Sundays, Tuesdays and

Thursdays. Have been limited writing others. The thing is that having had lousy weather, cold winds and rain for days, on top of that we were inoculated with 25cc of TT and 25cc of TAB, whatever they may be. One laddy passed out before he got the needle and one in our hut passed out as he stood talking during the afternoon. It gave me a rotten head, lousy backache and a hell of a temperature, besides a very tender arm and felt pretty rough and I don't feel so good today. In the afternoon I went off to bed and didn't get up until next morning, as I was on dental parade. It would have capped it all if I'd had to have many extractions. As it happened only one tooth was drilled and filled and another has to be done later. Don't worry dear, I'm feeling heaps better and the sun's trying to get out again. The only trouble is that we have another vaccination and inoculation in ten days' time, and a final inoculation a month after that.

In order to get an allowance for dependants, you have to make a voluntary one. This I did. I give 6d. (2½p), a day, 3s. 6d. a week, (17½p), but it has gone through for them and my parents are drawing 22s. 6d. (112½p), per week, which includes my 3s. 6d. Don't worry about cash for me. I hardly spend anything. We are still not allowed out of camp and beer being awful, I don't buy it. The only money we spend is on Blanco, Duraglit and Dubbin, etc.

No wireless in our hut. Don't worry about my feet being tender in these boots and I have some powder. We start on the square tomorrow, known round here as 'square bashing' and will not be getting our half day.

We are a mixed bag, very, but the majority are good lads. I haven't any special mates as yet, so I hang along with the Scots next to me. There are thirty in a hut, which is just a section. There are four sections in our party and so many parties to a company. We have been attending a lecture on things in general. Pride in the regiment, careless talk, use of lavatories, etc., and last but not least, a stern warning not to

12

mess about with the Elgin women when we do get out. From there, we marched to the quartermaster's stores to send our civvies home and are now waiting for the tea bugle. We also drew out rifles and bayonets and have to wear part of our webbing tomorrow on the square. So we are all blancoing for dear life! One section just passing out of their training, have marched back into camp after seventeen miles of it and didn't look so bad at that. Have been writing this letter off and on all day when I'd chance. As always, N.

All envelopes have to be re-used with stick-on labels. Stamps cost $2\frac{1}{2}$d. (1p).

12 June 1942

Well it's just on 9.30 p.m. and we have to be at our huts for roll-call at that time. If you are in, you answer, if you don't you'll be put down as out. If you are out, you have to report coming in or you are marked late and therefore on a charge. Here they all are, the lot, making up their beds and rather irate. We were bashing the square today – not half. Left, right. Oh and can the NCO shout!

We have had our first PT, two sets of rifle drill, a lecture by the CMS and party officer and by the padre. That was the end of the working day and since tea I've cleaned my boots and webbing, had supper and a shower, made my bed and now with you.

The place is in uproar. The Scotch element started it with 'When I get a pint on a Saturday night' and the Yorkshire lads jumped in with 'Ilkley Moor'. Then a soloist with a song about a 'Young lady up Bridge Street'. He comes from Barnsley. Then we've had a few Irish songs too.

I'm fine, top of the bill and enjoying life again. The morning was grand but the afternoon dull with showers and it isn't too warm. Since my shower and towelling, I've felt good. On the square again tomorrow and PT until 12.40 p.m. and then dinner. Rifle drill and lecture by the OC of 'C' Company. Then a lecture and the glorious pay parade, which is the first of my army career. We had a disappointment today and can't go out for another week, so not able to tell you about the district. The Scotch element are giving solos again and being howled down by the English. We are in the Scottish command. So if you see a rugged, bow-legged, haggis and porridge-eating Royal Engineer coming to meet you with a crooked smile and thistle in his hair, don't be surprised! Must close to the strains of 'Nelly Dean'! Yours always, N.

15 June 1942

Sunday morning about 10.45 a.m. and our NAAFI break, so instead of going for a drink and a bite, I wanted to start my weekend letter to you. We are late this morning and have only ten minutes and a full day's work to get through. At 11.05 a.m. we have to change from drill order to musketry order, then on rifles again, PT and dinner. After that there's a gas lecture, more rifles and of course, square bashing until tea 5.15 p.m. Then I shall clean up for tomorrow and finish this letter.

I have had a letter from Brand, our club secretary, with a form to complete for the Legion and enclosed was a postal order from the Village Residents for 7s. 6d., (37½p). So now I have more money than I came with. So don't you worry about my financial affairs.

It has been a hectic day. We always have to parade 5 minutes before time. After tea, I managed to do a bit of washing, but still have under-clothes and socks to do. I'll be quite a dab-hand soon. The food is fairly good here, but such a scramble and all on one plate, tea in a basin, and wash your own cutlery. The meals have variety. For breakfast the usual porridge or cereals and either bacon, liver or scrambled eggs. Dinner is meat pie, steak, fish, both fresh and canned, and usual vegetables. Then always jam and puddings. So I've said, it's a right royal fight to get it and such a smell of grease. I should get 2s., (10p), a day, 14s., (70p), a week. Sometimes there are stoppages for breakages and things and only got 12 bob (60p) last week. The lads are arriving. A couple of Scots wrestling on the floor and language not too good. N.

17 June 1942

What a day! Up as usual and on the square bright and early. A great six foot bloke with a row of ribbons like a row of scarlet runner beans and an arm with stripes, bombs and crown all down it. He drilled us round and round, up and down, right turn, left turn, about turn, halt, slow march, quick march, open order march, mark time, slope arms, present and order arms. In fact he almost broke our arms. Our feet are sore and shoulders skinned with banging it on the 'present'. In a full day of sunshine, for a change, finished at 5.15 p.m. for tea, but we were kept back as we were last and all was about eaten up. Managed some at last.

We had to prepare our kit for inspection laid out on the bed as per diagram on wall. Palliasse turned back, blankets folded 'so', valise, haversack, respirator, tin hat, net and sandbag, cleaning gear and brushes and spare clothes. This had to be done by 6.30 p.m. It was 9.00 p.m. by the time the officer came and was off after fifteen minutes, two and a half hours late. Last night we got half an hour extra drill on the square for being two minutes late on parade. We had arranged a football match for the evening – that was of no consequence!

15

No, I'm not homesick, but feel very browned off being bossed about by dozens of jumped up NCOs. Thanks for sending me a watch. It will be very handy, as you have no idea how we have to work to the minute.

There's one chap here stitching his trouser behind and two more putting on buttons and all the rest giving advice; although it's very funny, it is not very polite! As always, N.

19 June 1942

It's the 10.30 a.m. NAAFI break. Instead of going there I'm writing to you. We are at last getting our long awaited half-day and may not have a chance to write to you later. We are allowed out until 11.59 p.m., but I'm not contemplating being out so late. I need to do some shopping. I need two dusters, two brushes and hair cream and I also want to post my Civil Defence gas mask home. After tea I'll be out again looking for a decent pub and a pint.

We have a new party coming in today. Some have already arrived. Wonder if there will be anybody I know. Poor buggers, they little know what they are in for.

I have written to Jack and Rose A but not any of the lads yet. I've two letters from Mum to answer. Uncle Will from Blackpool is staying. Mum still misses me, she says.

I've income tax papers to fill up but have explained they are locked up at home. Remember the chap who I worked on the docks with? He writes from Newton Abbot saying there's a job for me at a little shipyard on the River Dart if I apply straight away. It's building mine sweepers. Ironical isn't it and I'm afraid just too late.

Time to fall in. I have been on the square first thing after

16

porridge and sausages. Two sets at rifle drill, now we start again on gas drill, PT and dinner. After which, we parade for inspection prior to being let out.

10.30 p.m. Well I've been out for the first time and find Elgin quite a nice little place. It's a cross between Beverley and York with old-fashioned buildings in stone and cobbled streets. The same multiple of shops and people and many, many service men and women. A Scotch laddy and me had tea then on to the pictures – *Bad Man at Dakota* – not bad. We had some supper at the Church of Scotland canteen, then fish and chips at a cafe. Then back home, or rather 'jail'. Must close. As always, N.

22 June 1942

We've had a half day. I had an hour's lie down and then blancoed and have dressed since dinner and been out for tea at a place the service lads use. It was a long queue, but a good meal – two plates of chips and pie or fish and bread and butter with two cups of tea. All for the sum of 1s. (5p). I went for a walk, had a pint, another walk, then another pint. I finished with supper at the Church of Scotland and back to camp at 9.30 p.m.

I've sent cards to your folk and the lads. Seems to have been a lazy day today. An instruction lecture and a three mile run, which nearly killed me, but I managed it. Hope you aren't feeling too lonely. Treat yourself to something. Our reveille is at 6.30 a.m. I generally sneak an extra quarter of an hour if the corporal doesn't see me. If he does it's out sharp or get tipped out. So it's shave, wash and dress for breakfast at 7.15 a.m. prompt.

Now next day, Sunday. I had liver this morning. On the square in the rain on small arms practice. This afternoon full time on same. Tonight the dance band is playing for two hours in the NAAFI. Next Wednesday an ENSA (Entertainment National Service Association) concert in the gym.

After dinner and when eating it, we were systematically dive-bombed by fighters. No bombs, but they didn't half shake the place as they screamed down. I haven't said this for a long time and so I'd better say it now – I am still very much in love with you and miss you terribly. Yesterday we were told we probably wouldn't get leave until training is finished in five months. N.

Card   23 June 1942

Excuse card. Have had second inoculations and vaccination. Under the weather but got your letter this dinner time, one from home and Wing. Will write Thursday. N.

25 June 1942

I'm champion today and in harness and on the square this morning. After break, Gas and PT and half day off. I'm a bit light in the pocket until pay tomorrow, having lived it up last week. Contrary to expectations, the ENSA concert last night was a damn good show. There were two comedians, one comedienne, three singers and dancers and compere, who was a ventriloquist, a tenor and a lovely lassie who sang very appealingly and brought the house down, bless her.

It may seem paltry (yet not in these times), but I had my first taste of pinching. We have drying rooms after doing our washing, and now I only have one pair of socks left and one handkerchief. The habit is to pinch someone else's. It isn't in me to do so and will have to get more out of my credits. I've just received your parcel and letter. Thanks a lot and for the aspirin and cascara. It will be useful when needed.

It's a glorious day and we are stripped to the waist doing PT. What a picture – some scabby thin, thick short, stocky, long, lean and moderate. Some now laid out sunning themselves. If you would be good enough, as you suggested, would you pop over to Mum's and get my tax papers. You have a key to my effects. I'd be very pleased to have them. As always, N.

29 June 1942

It's Saturday night. No letters since Thursday. After square bashing this morning, we had unarmed combat, ordered and instilled by the instructor, telling us to kick and bite at every possible moment, especially his teeth and 'luggage'. We had a sports meeting this afternoon. I failed to qualify. Went into Elgin after tea, had a pint and walk. My mate went to the dance and I came back to write to you. I'm in bed and popping off as soon as I've written more.

There's an intersection football match tomorrow night. I don't know if I'm playing – a team may already be picked. Monday night we have a concert of local talent. We have a gas test on tomorrow. You will remember it from your gas training. A nose and throat irritant generally odourless and undetectable. It makes you sneeze and your eyes run, cough and sickness. This is the point – on no account must we take our respirator off, but blow out through the air outlet valve. We look like having an enjoyable session. Had a letter from cousin Jack, who asked after you again and had rooms for us whenever we liked to go.

19

My mother has sent me a white bread cake and a boiling of new potatoes. I did enjoy them and shared them with the others, but one said he had never seen them cooked that way before and declined.

I'll tell you what I could do with sometime, that's clean dusters or rags – you could wrap them up round anything you are likely to send. On Sunday, after a dinner of beef, mash and the inevitable beans, bread pudding and custard, we had the usual square bashing, bayonet training, PT and the dreaded gas. We had to line up in twenties, take off our masks for two minutes in this room, then replace masks and off outside where they ran us round for ten minutes to make our lungs work overtime and breath the good air in. What a sight. Some had swollen faces, coughing and sneezing, eyes and noses running. The noise was like a symphony orchestra tuning up. All the same, it's a lousy feeling. I had a tightening and irritation in my lungs and swelling in my throat, with saliva in profusion. I've a lousy headache still. I'm not ashamed to say that I finished up on my hands and knees dead beat, along with the majority. It must be the worst death possible.

Whilst on about death, I haven't got my will made out yet.

I didn't have the faintest urge to go dancing last night but preferred to write to you. I'm always true. Bye, N.

1 July 1942

NAAFI break again. The army have provided me with a 'housewife', so I don't need anything in that line, but if you can get me some grey wool for darning, I'd be grateful. No ill effects from the gas. I was OK by night. We went through the bayonet assault course on Monday, what a do! At the double all the way, in shirt sleeves yelling like mad, sticking dummies and climbing over a fifteen foot fence, drop down and stick the dummy. At the double up a slope, drop into a ditch, stick the dummy, run along a rail twenty yards under cover and stick into a trench, fire five rounds, up and down into a shell crater, up a slope, over a tree, over a wall every twenty yards, sticking dummies all the time, into a sand pit and more dummies. We then collapsed for a rest. One lad smashed his rifle, one got his bayonet fast in a tree, one stuck another in the chin. I managed to fill my rifle with sand and knock a yard of skin off my hand and stagger on.

After tea.

What a miserable tea we had – cocoa, bread, jam, one piece of lettuce with a bit of salmon on top. They've had it in for us today, so we have to go on the square again at 6 p.m. for a further period of drill. We aren't up to standard and I believe we have to pass it by next week. No respite after cleaning up ready for tomorrow. Your Sunday's letter arrived at dinner time. Thanks for it and the labels. The weather is rainy. We've had our first lecture on MP, (map reading), also know your enemy, a series about the German armed forces. Mother is going to Chester for a week and Aunt Emma will be looking after Dad and May who is still lodging and now in work. Must away until Thursday. Bye and kisses, N.

3 July 1942

What a scorcher yesterday! We nearly burned up. Today looks like being the same. It's our half day, so I expect I'll have tea out and go to the pictures. Whilst I remember, you did ask if there's anything I wanted and you would get it if possible. I don't like asking, you will know that, but I'd like one or two shaving brushes and two small brushes for my nails and polishing buttons. I know they can be expensive or rare to get.

It's lovely and sunny and we've had the best dinner since

being here. We have been on the miniature range. I was a washout. We were firing the anti-tank rifle at a moving tank target. The MO has given us another health inspection. My vaccination area is infected and being treated. Got your Tuesday's letter at dinner and the postage stamps. You must not spend your money on me unless I specifically ask for anything. The fact that you are keeping the bank account going is appreciated. Jack A.'s letter said our poplar trees and blackcurrants are doing well.

Hope to pass off the square Wednesday. Wish me luck and that I don't drop my rifle again! Cheerio, take care, N.

We managed to by a third of an acre of land for building on after the war.

6 July 1942

I've been on conservancy duty this morning, as so many are each Saturday and having had to see the MO, thought I'd take today as my period. The MO's orderly treats us, a corporal, not too clean, but a good chap for all that. I told you about my arm being painful and septic after vaccination and I have been having an anti-flo poultice on. Now it's something like vaseline and expect it's OK for healing.

No letter from anybody yesterday. I'm hoping for a bundle this dinner time. It's the morning break and after on the square, we have our Saturday run, then dinner and half day, of course. We have to clean up ready for Sunday and this we have now done. Since dinner I've scrubbed the hut out, washed windows, dusted the roof principles, ledges, lockers, dado, entrance and porch, washed and stoned the steps, scrubbed the rifle rack, washed lamp shades and bulbs, black-leaded the stove and pipes. Outside weeded the borders and swept the path.

Finally, my mate and I went into Elgin, had tea and a half pint, then a walk right out of town westwards, towards Inverness, I believe, and came across the River Lossie and a beautiful old stone bridge and sat down and studied nature. It had turned out quite hot and we saw trout in abundance, a pair of wagtails and large thrushes, at least one little wren and some finches and I thought I saw a yellowhammer. Wish you had been here. We stayed about two hours before returning to Elgin and back here after having tea at the Church of Scotland canteen. On our run this morning, I noticed several fields of cocked hay. The roadsides are lined with wild roses and my mind flies back to a river bank and hours of happiness with a lovely person. Had your Tuesday's letter this dinner time.

The stores orderly found a pair of socks he thought could be mine, one sock was new the other three inches shorter!

Sunday NAAFI Break

Have been on the square again 11 'til 1 p.m. and put through it with the Senior Drill Instructor, a bloke with a voice like a foghorn, a chest like a barrel and a bite like caustic soda – what a man – but by hell we did it! Rifle drill it was and I've a lump on the side of my head like an egg from the barrel, skin off my thumb and collarbone red-raw. Still we did it. It was so very hot the tar was melting on the roads. We were baked. One chap collapsed on the square this morning due to his vaccination. I asked the corporal if I could see the MO this morning. He refused and said I'd to go in my own time. Bugger me, I got it in their time. I've quite a few to write to, at least eight, which includes my former boss. All for now. Love, N.

NAAFI break and what a break! Yesterday when I came in off map reading, I found that my bedding had been disturbed, my battle dress in a heap. Obviously someone had gone through the pockets, but glory be, I'd left nothing in them. Today I was second in the hut and found a bloke inside. The corporal's suit was hanging out of the window. Anyhow, the bloke has been reported and a charge brought against him and we've been in front of the OC. So I suppose he will be tried and found guilty. The best of it is he was being posted to another unit today. There are two watches missing and if we hadn't caught him, he'd have been away and suspicion placed on all of us.

You ought to have seen us last night preparing for the big day pass out. We were up until midnight when the CSM came in and caught us and gave us a good telling off and the corporal got it in the neck and reported to the OC. We had a laddy cutting our hair and we had won an electric iron from a bloke, so we were all pressing our suits.

After dinner yesterday we were on top of the hills map reading, setting out the points – roads, railways, churches and mountains and getting from one point to another. The ground was lovely and springy on the mossy turf. We crossed the Lossie on a rope bridge and noticed a pair of swans and four young sailing along without a care. That was the first time we had been out training. Next week we go on the ranges. Must away, Love, N.

It's only Wednesday night but thought I'd best get started in case I don't get much time tomorrow and in order to tell you about our 'pass off'. We passed all right, but what a to do. We had been busy cleaning our equipment on the Tuesday night and this morning we were up and dressed on parade for inspection by our officer at 9 a.m. We marched on the square and started the ball rolling. Dead on 10 a.m. the CO and his officers marched on and we came to attention. He came down and inspected individually. What an inspection! Every man of us, fronts and backs, nothing missed. This took an hour and each section had to do our stuff in front of them. All our section, being No. 1, were first, as we always are, even at pay parade. I'm about in the middle of the front rank – right under their noses or that's how I feel. Eventually we were passed in review order for the CO's speech. We made a few mistakes, but he passed us as one of the best parties he had seen and hoped we would keep it up at all times. We then marched off to be complimented by our OC and finally dismissed. The strain was a bit tense. Exactly two hours of drill and stiff attention, not batting an eyelid and we were ready for an easy.

We were due to have map reading on the hills this afternoon, but it teemed with rain and instead had an indoor session and on the miniature range till teatime. No letters today, but had a parcel from Aunt Louie and my mate got one from home which we have just eaten, his of buns and scones, lovely home-made food. We will be eating mine tomorrow. My arm has given no further trouble, just an elastoplast from the ones you sent. We were to have a photograph today of our section and company. Will let you know if it comes off.

After dinner now and our half day, but have to stand by in case I'm wanted as a witness to this 'pinching' and also to draw our second battle dress. The Lord knows if I'll get out! Love, N.

13 July 1942

Saturday night and a few lines in case tomorrow is a busy day. We are confined to barracks till further notice – there is a big invasion scheme on. All ranks are either in camp as a reserve or out attacking the enemy. We get breakfast tomorrow morning and draw rations for the day, so bang goes Sunday dinner.

We had two periods of PT and went out for our run only much further. Up the valley and over the hills, crossing and re-crossing the river Lossie dozens of times, by trees, real rope hand-over-hand. All this was done in brilliant sunshine, soft spongy grass, fern and bracken, whole patches of forget-me-nots and banks of violets still in bloom and the wild roses in all their glory. We went through a big estate away from the river and passed a whitewashed farm house with a winding drive of bushes and shrubs. I was sorry to come back into captivity.

A letter from JA says our poplars are ten feet high. Dad says the pear tree is dropping its pears unripe. I had to buy a stiff-backed exercise book and a pen for red ink the other day; 3s. 9d. (19p) and 3d. (1p) – blimey! We only get 14s. (70p) a week. No, I'm afraid having passed out on the square doesn't mean we will get leave. We start on the range at Lossiemouth this time next week – don't know if it's daily or under canvas – at least it will be interesting. We only get twenty minutes for NAAFI break and in that time I manage to change from one order to another and I prefer to write to you. I'm not a snob – the tea is lousy and I cannot stand the pushing, shoving and wrestling. It's the same at meal time.

Sunday after tea

What a busy day, burning sun – my face is as sore as a baby's bottom! First thing on the square, then lecture, then battle order and off to the range. Firing all morning and grenades in the afternoon. They are called Mills bombs, but we have to say HE36. They are cut like a pineapple and go off on a four second fuse from releasing the pin, so you throw high in an overhand way and then duck. We all threw one each. One lad dropped his over the firing pit. The instructor pushed it a bit further. It fell behind the wall. Off it went and nobody hurt. The instructor spoke gently to the lad and made him throw another. Our tin hats get red hot with the sun. There are no trees or shelter anywhere. We had demonstrations of the Molotov cocktail – a fearsome thing of nitric acid and sugar. There's one that goes off like a roman candle, which besides burning, gives off dense smoke. Sorry if I bore you with all this about me. I tell you as I think you will like to know it seems to make me closer to you. Until Tuesday. All yours, N.

15 July 1942

I have been out at Lossiemouth all day and found your letter, one from Dad, Mother at Chester and Wing when I got in. We set off at 8 a.m. and returned at 6 p.m. We travelled on an army bus – a truck with coal, dixies, wood, cocoa, ammunition, bren guns, telephones and target markers. We disembarked half a mile from the range which is on the sand dunes, looking out north to the sea. What a scene! Miles of scrub bushes, gravel, sparse grass and heather. We commenced on the hundred yards range with five rounds. They don't half kick. My score fifteen out of a possible twenty. After moving back to two hundred yards, again I scored fifteen out of a possible twenty at the bull. Then five rounds on the target which only lasts or shows for four seconds and you have to plaster it. Mine was a washout. Going three hundred yards back and five rounds now with respirator on. We retired and boiled our rifles out. Six to eight pints of boiling water down the barrel. We had had a break for dinner which was haversack rations we had taken. Ready for tea we had a buster for a change. Stew, mash and turnips, rice pudding and prunes. Having finished square bashing it's range work later. All love, N.

16 July 1942

NAAFI break

Thanks for the parcel which arrived yesterday. The yellow duster and bits of frock, how they bring back memories! Thanks for the brushes, writing paper and envelopes. This is the last two pages on which I'm writing, so you have hit just right. We've had another grand day on the range and tea when we got in. Our breakfast was awful – cocoa with neither sugar or milk. There was nothing palatable, so I ended up with dry bread and scrambled egg substitute. I'm looking forward to getting a meal out. It's our half day today, if we get it. After tea at 5.20 p.m. we had to report to the company office for an interview. I stood until 7.15 p.m. and was told to come back at 8.15 p.m. We dashed back to clean ourselves up and our rifles etc, then dashed back again. It was 9.30 p.m. when I got back, having been told I wasn't wanted at all, as there had been a mix-up. An officer there did ask me about my trade grade. We now expect to be trade tested for reposting when a unit needs making up. Tradesmen should get extra pay. It could mean £2 a week.

Today after dinner, we have to parade for a telling off about dirty billets. We don't know what was dirty only three towels folded wrong, bang will go our half day again. These half days are only a myth. No post so far. The NCO hasn't yet bothered to issue. Thank goodness I've got you to belly ache to! Bye and kisses, N.

We have had a good dinner today – meat pie, two veg and mash, then rice pudding and fruit. The big shots were round from the CO to lowly sergeant. We have actually finished for the day, but it's awfully dull and cold.

No post for me today either. We had our usual conservancy period this morning and two lectures, then an interesting lecture by a civilian on Japan, their nature and morals and a rough sketch of their war history. I'm feeling very fit after doing PT every day. We are on field craft next week so I will be pretty tired at the end of the day.

It's now Sunday and I called at the tailors to get my battledress tunic altered. Then I went along into Elgin and looked around Woolworths and bought some hair cream. I had tea and then went to the pictures to see *The Chocolate Soldier* with Nelson Eddy and somebody called Rise Stevens. The singing was lovely – it made me think of you. I met some of the lads and had a drink with them. Had some supper and back to camp and bed at 10.00 p.m. Keep smiling and your hair as I love it. All yours, N.

23 July 1942

We had the Seaforth Highlands Band in the gym last night. It was marvellous – wish you had been there. Eighteen men and bandmaster in full Highland dress. A baritone sang several ballads and Scottish songs, including 'Hill Caledonian' 'Scotland Forever' and a beautiful rendering of 'I'll Walk Beside You'. Poor sentimental me nearly cried! Beautiful Strauss waltzes, pipers and dancers, light musical comedy, finishing with a swing-band.

I got your Sunday's letter yesterday and hoping for one tomorrow.

We have been 'flitted' into a similar hut, but minus beds and we're having to sleep on the floor. It is said we will soon be going to Findhorn pontooning. Maybe I'll learn to swim.

My moustache is getting out of hand, would you get me a pair of scissors that are small with blunt ends, please? Annie Proctor gave me the ones I have and asked for a halfpenny. Also, could you make me a bag about a foot square with a draw string.

We've had a laddie die. His body has been sent home to Leeds for burial. Four Leed's lads have gone as bearers. We spent 25s. (£1.25), on a wreath and a small bit of cash for his wife. Very sad. Must away, As always, N.

Letters from home is the most important thing in a serviceman's life. Irregularity in receiving the letters was no fault of the sender. During hostilities delays occurred, but almost every letter in our case got through.

17 August 1942

Thanks for the scissors, just right and sharp. The cake you sent has gone down well with only a corner left. Mother had sent one and I'll let you into a secret, I'd to cut it to put it in your tin box and in making comparisons it wasn't as moist and dark as yours.

I've written and thanked my late boss for the security locks he sent, (he had asked if I wanted anything), one for my locker and one for my kit bag and they are smashers.

My economy labels are all used and writing paper about finished and hope to get some more when next out.

Thursday night we were out on the scheme, which I mentioned to you. We marched five miles there and back. Blew up a bridge near Lossiemouth. We started at 9.00 p.m. and got back about 3.30 a.m. Flat out again. Only two nights in bed this week.

This morning we haven't done a great deal, but I've been re-vaccinated. So I hope it will have taken this time. I may get out to the pictures tonight, meanwhile, must try and get a shut eye for a couple of hours.

Sunday morning

For a change it's showing promise of a sunny day and I hope not too hot, as it's enough carrying pack and rifle. There we go 'outside'.

After tea

The day has kept fine, but a cold wind. We have been busy with 'knobs and lashings' and have had a late dinner of beef, veg and rice pud, though insufficient. I'd no mail on Saturday, so looking forward to Monday when I get in. I did go out last night, but there was such a crowd waiting to see *Smiling Through* that instead I went and had a couple of pints. Some of the lads had seen the film and said how good it was in technicolour, with Jeannet MacDonald and Brian Aherne. So recommend it to you. Until Tuesday dear. Goodbye my love, N.

20 August 1942

I'm out of writing paper until I go into town today, so please excuse this short note on one of your letter cards. We had an inspection by the OC this morning and church parade, then our last inoculation and I hope for a half day. Yes, I too miss our weekends together. Seems years ago since you were welcoming me to your Mum's home. I wonder when again.

So, you are going to Keighley. I don't quite know where it is. So wondering if you will get home as regularly or how far for me to go and see you. Perhaps you will be able to get time off if I get leave. I cannot expect money from you, you know that, and I'll get my tax paid somehow. So you've been to a pub! You won't get drunk and let anyone take advantage. I'd hate that.

I've written home to notify of your visit for the income tax papers. I am very happy you are going. Take a look at 'Hideaway' and taking Betty, I hope she likes it as much as we do. Cheerio, N.

The visit to a pub was a one off with a friend and Air Force husband who wanted to meet me and we played darts, which I was very good at then. Later N. was to find me an embarrassment at functions and having a tomato juice was all I needed! C.

22 August 1942

The farmers are busy cutting corn round here. What a day Thursday! After all our trials, we were marched into Elgin for the swimming display and when we got there, complete with towels and things, there wasn't room for us, so we were dismissed. I had a look round and bought this horrible writing paper, an ice-cream and walked back to camp. After tea I went back into Elgin and saw *Four Feathers* in colour. You would enjoy it. It was nearly 11.00 p.m. when I got back. On signing in I received your parcel of notepaper and toothpaste, Macleans of course! Got your Wednesday letter tonight with razor blades and stick-on labels. Again many thanks.

I know you have volunteered to pay any of my tax owing – if any – and that you would draw out your superannuation to help, it's no go, dear. One of our lads comes from Keighley and tells me it's a Poor Law institution with midwifery, but you will be telling me all about it when you get there tomorrow.

My second vaccination doesn't seem to have taken, but hasn't troubled me like before. I'm pleased your vaccination has been OK. We have some Indians in training back in the mountains up here and a lot of Norwegians too. Big blonde fellows, fine chaps of all ages, speaking a little English. Engineers, of course, so it makes one wonder about this invasion business – I wonder!

Saturday afternoon

Variable weather. We are out on a scheme tomorrow. A battalion exercise but what exactly don't know. I hope the weather is fine. I am sending this letter on to Keighley so it will be a surprise and greeting for you. All love, N.

26 August 1942

Tuesday morning

Having just come off guard, washed and got ready for the day and patiently waiting for the others to go for our late breakfast. We don't get it until 8.30 a.m. after guard duty and start work at 9.45 a.m. It was a lovely night after a grand day, but today it's dull with slight drizzle. I didn't get a letter from you Friday or Saturday. I expect you were very busy moving to your new quarters. The laddie I spoke to you about lives at Silsden. He's the one who told me about the hospital and he says his home is three miles away – a sixpenny bus ride and can put me up, should we not get our leave together. My longed-for leave!

Cousin Jessie has sent me a jar of jam and a chocolate cake.

After breakfast

We have a few more minutes before joining the others on field works. For breakfast we managed to bag two lots of bacon, plenty of bread and butter and I took Jessie's jam. So for once I'm full up to the top.

I don't know if I told you that the programme has changed. We go to Gillston instead of Findhorn, marching each way, morning and night. This course is to last ten days. Hope it isn't far and the weather fine. They brought a laddie into our cells last night. One out of the party who came two weeks after us. He had run away twice so evidently doesn't like this life. It must be lousy in the cells. We had to take supper in to them last night and although they have a bed, I shudder to think what it's like in there, with the door banged shut and the bolt shot. Will have to close now dear, it's time for off. So I'm looking forward to a letter tonight.

26 August 1942

It's Thursday and a beautiful one too. It was the same yesterday and we were able to strip off. I hope it continues after so many indifferent days. I hope you are getting your fair share. Yesterday I had your first letter from Keighley and you will have received mine. Sorry to know that you are not impressed, probably because it's strange and you don't know anyone. Why did you leave the last post? (*I was delegated there by the Powers*).

After dinner

And quite a good one. As far as we can gather about leave, dear, we expect it about 21 October. That's 8 weeks time and in other words two bloody months! Let me have your phone number to hand. I much appreciate your kind words of the things I was able to help you with. They all recall happy times and the thrill it gave me to buy you things. Will have to close now as we are about ready for off. Love, N.

29 August 1942

Saturday and NAAFI break

We had our swimming lesson on Thursday afternoon. It was grand, the water lovely and clean, changing all the time at a regular temperature. We had to jump in. What a jump I made – right under and then to carry out the land-drill we had been taught. We pushed off and to glide I swallowed half the bath as soon as I lost my legs. I believe I'll swim in the end. Anyhow, I thoroughly enjoyed it. In the afternoon I went out and saw a film with William Powell and Myrna Loy in *Shadow of the Thin Man*. After having tea and two pints of beer, I was in by 9.00 p.m. with $7\frac{1}{2}$d. left. (3p).

I've had a lovely parcel of sweet red apples from Eva and Tom who are holidaying in Lincolnshire. Bless their hearts. Especially Eva's; I'd no idea she cared so much. Yesterday we were at Gillston which is a very small loch. It took an hour's march out and in, so imagine about four miles. We had two lectures and made an assault bridge which we had to run over. Two of the lads fell in! We launched and manned a rubber dinghy and an assault boat in which there sits the commander, two oarsmen, two riflemen, two oarsmen, two riflemen and away you go. We are only there until next Friday when we march to Findhorn for pontooning.

This morning we have had a period of internal economy and now on TOETS, (Test of Elementary Trainings). Then we had a drill period and a Saturday morning run. Then half day. There's no post again and I haven't heard from you since Wednesday, so I hope you are all right. Bye, N.

35

On Saturday night I received a letter from you when I got back. I'd already posted my Sunday epistle early on – it's the time and opportunity here, and dispatch and delivery within the camp and I didn't want to disappoint you. Thanks for yours, now I'm looking forward to one tomorrow. I just cannot help my clamour for your letters.

So at last you have got recognition for your abilities and how grand to be awakened by a cup of tea. (I could just do with a good cuppa). You will be busy preparing the theatre and wards so I hope you have an efficient staff. This striking paper is from Woolworths and although I don't like it, I must use it up. Excuse the vividness!

I didn't know, until you mentioned it, that you saw *The Four Feathers* with John Clements and Ralph Richardson when you were fourteen. You say it was also called *Beau Geste*, meaning 'Beautiful Gesture' and that its memory will last all your life. Many thanks for the income tax papers. Pleased to know that the hideaway is still perfect. I'd wondered how it looked now.

It was lousy weather on Sunday and not so good Monday. The sun did come out and was awfully hot and didn't we sweat. Still busy at Gillston daily. Back at night for tea and lovely hot showers and a concert by the locals, which was very good. Plenty of dirty jokes and hearty singing by all present. I managed to write to Wing before the concert. Today we have been on the loch again, ferrying lorries across and back. By 4.00 p.m. to a medical inspection by the MO, (the rude inspection).

Tomorrow we are out all day and night bridging across the lock in darkness. So I hope I don't drop in. As far as I can gather we clean up and finish at Gillston, then come back and pack up for Findhorn and march there on Friday. We will then have all of Saturday off, or so I'm told. The work there is very hard and heavy, but short hours.

4 September 1942

Thursday night

Quite a panic on. We are in the midst of packing for the journey to Findhorn tomorrow. We were out all day at Gillston on Wednesday as I told you we would be. Then we started bridging and when a car was driven over it and it was inspected, down it all came. We got back about 1.00 a.m. Contrary to expectations, we had to be up at reveille as usual and we've been at Gillston all day again. Since tea we've had a pay parade and I've had a haircut, packed half my stuff and now I'm jiggered. All our belongings have to go with us, all our bedding, in fact everything. I don't know where I'm going to put it. There are boots, coats and mess tins and socks flying in all directions. Still need a shower, then supper and I'll write a letter home.

Had your nice long Saturday's letter last night and very pleased to note that with each letter you are liking things better. The weather remains very mixed and cold. My most pressing need is sleep to make up for last night's loss and the march tomorrow. I see you are going great guns in the tennis tournament. I'm wishing you all the luck and with the preparations and getting shipshape. Wink O was on *The Liverpool*, but no further news of him. Do make arrangements for my leave so that you can freely get away when the time comes. I'd let you know straight away. Must away. All love, N.

Findhorn

Another phase in my army career. There's no change in the address as the mail comes via Pinefield. We are now at Findhorn, glorious Findhorn. I'm told the original place is sunk underneath the sand. (Years and years ago of course). I can quite believe it, as there are miles and miles of it – sand hills and dunes. Anyhow, to keep things in order and answer your letter, thanks for trying to get me some Yardley's hair cream. I have tried without success and given up hope, though I have a tin somewhere which I can use when with you.

Matron is an old so and so, then. It's funny, they all seem to be. I suppose they get that way, like our NCOs. It's the power of their position to crack the whip. If you object you may gain a point or get the hammer – we usually get the hammer! Remind your Dad that I'm due a letter. On Friday we set off to march about 8.30 a.m. All went well until we had to do a scheme crawling across the heather, taking up positions and attacking a wood held by the enemy. This caused a lot of exertion and, not content with that, we had two dive bombing attacks and a further hour of it until dinner. Then up again and we reached here about 4.00 p.m., tired but glad to be sorted out and collected our gear and installed ourselves in a little tent. There are nine of us and equipment and we are as warm as toast. We had tea and the food is very good. There are two cooks and a fatigue party does the rough work each day.

After the excitement of the day, I was on night guard with its howling wind and sand blowing all over the place. Saturday we had a lecture and general tidying up and I was able to have a pint before dinner at 2.00 p.m. and slept all afternoon. After tea I went out for a pint and singsong and then early to bed. This morning we have been learning to row cutters and pontoons in the bay. The weather is cold and we get only a little sunshine. We are in the sea all day, launching and pushing off in just sand shoes (no socks) and gym shorts or with trousers turned up to the knees. A jacket and tin hat completes the lot. There's water up to the knees, sometimes the waist. On the whole it's good fun and I am enjoying it here. I'll describe the place later on, but it's a small place with three pubs, two hotels and a very small quay.

There is also a Church of Scotland canteen. No pubs open tonight, the Sabbath is strictly observed up here. We had some excitement this afternoon; a couple of seals came right up into the bay. The bosses-that-be had a shot at them. We are told there is 10s. (50p) a piece on them to keep them down, as they eat all the herring. I'm pleased they didn't get hit as they rolled about on a sandbank, sunning themselves.

I had a letter from Stan today. He's on holiday in Edinburgh. He says Bill is with him for the day. I take it as being Wink O. Until Tuesday dear, N.

9 September 1942

Tuesday afternoon

What a post I had last night – yours and five others. Betty wrote a nice letter and enclosed 2s. 6d. ($12\frac{1}{2}$p), worth of stamps. We are still busy in and out of the water. After posting your letter on Sunday, I went for a cup of tea and a cake in the Church of Scotland canteen and we had a singsong amongst about half a dozen well known hymns. A little old lady said a prayer for us.

The post office here is a house-cum-shop, rather quaint. We were up at 6.30 a.m. this morning and on the beach at 7.30 a.m. doing PT and in the water to finish off – and wasn't it cold! This morning we have been ferrying the Argyle and

Sutherland Light Infantry across the bay in a mock attack. Machine guns going, trench mortars sending over smoke-shells as a screen against our landings, everything very realistic. Just been told to go for cigs and chocolate ration. Will be with you again later. Went for a ramble on the beach as I'm skint and now rather tired and early to bed. All love, N.

11 September 1942

Thursday

After a rifle examination, we marched to Kinloss for a period of drill in the 'drome square. This afternoon we have a football match against the NCOs. So, you have been having invasion exercises. I know it wouldn't be easy for you, intruding into this responsible job and I know you will be capable of doing it well and for the cause.

The lads had a darts match with the locals last night and on winning got free beer. Never mind, there'll come a day – I was too low on cash to go out. I have said the food was good here and it is, but our hard work makes us ravenous, so if we can buy a loaf and some jam, we reckon on going out in search. This morning I was cleaning out my rifle when there was a heck of a scurry. A little wagtail flashed by, frightened to death. On its tail was a big brown hawk which we scared off and the little blighter got away.

About half an hour ago three destroyers steamed up, presumably for Invergordon, which was the place from which the Duke of Kent set out on his ill-fated journey, we are told. It was the port also where the ships of the fleet mutinied a few years back on account of insufficient food ration, I seem to remember. The wind has got up to galeforce. The locals say it isn't always like that – it sometimes snows! We've had quite a job to control pontooning, the wind and tide tossing them all over the place and the seas breaking over them, Love, N.

This place was so unfriendly, I contacted the 'powers' and asked that they would let the matron and staff acknowledge my position. This they did and things improved somewhat. I had some lovely auxillaries learning their job and to break the monotony of war-time, we went on rambles, along with some of the night staff I mixed with when relieving.

23 September 1942

Morning break, Tuesday

This morning we are to have lectures in a hut on the Inglis Bridge at the other side of the camp. The weather is at its worst, raining for days, and we've been soaked each day and having to wear battledress instead of denims. I've no manners at all now. I only think in numbers one, two, three and left, right, left. So if I inspect you by numbers and grab all the food on the table, then walk off to wash my knife, fork and spoon and go into the backyard and shave, please forgive me.

I'll be pleased to have some more of the scones and cheese that you sent. My many thanks. *How Green Was My Valley* by Richard Llewelyn MP, one of the most useful MPs, is a film I've longed to see now that you remind me as having seen it.

Sorry I didn't write to you on Thursday. On Sunday we started on the Bailey bridge. It rained all day and in the evening I started to try to write up notes. I've got all the Gillston and Findhorn and all the bridging notes yet to start on. Tomorrow I'll have to write home and then write to you on Thursday. I'll also have to write to Stan and tell him about the trains. It's only about a month now dear, so wait patiently. Always yours, N.

A gap in letters shows N back at Elgin and under a great deal of pressure.

26 September 1942

Thursday

Our officer had told us that we are going on leave on 21 October.

There is an argument going on between the English and Scots about Bannockburn and Flodden Field. We have been on water supply lectures all morning and practical in the afternoon. We've learnt how to obtain water and treat it for human consumption. The REs are responsible for the whole water supply of the said army. The subject is far-reaching and we have literally pages of notes on it.

We have conservancy and church parade this morning. We also have our swimming for non-swimmers. I'll be glad to have a break at the pictures. I'm going to see *Next of Kin* and then return to write up more notes. Our water project continues for about another week and then we go on to earthworks, i.e. barbed wiring, trenches, weapon slits, camouflage and so forth. Next will be revision exams and then leave, that glorious long-awaited leave!

A letter from home informed me that Mum had taken Uncle Will and Dad to Blackpool and Dad had messed his bunkers. She seemed generally fed-up, if that's anything fresh. Jack said they would put fruit bushes in for us on the plot.

Must close, the big noises are coming round to inspect the huts.

After dinner

Two hundred and fifty plus at the Church parade plus NCOs. We have voluntary church parades on Sundays or PT. It's hellish cold. We will soon be getting an extra blanket and issue of woollen underclothes. Rumour has it that we are to get 3d. (1p) per day trade pay. So I hope there is some back pay to come. Bye love, N.

28 September 1942

We have just come in from our Saturday run and it was quite a long one, but grand. It's very cold today. Before the run we saw *Next of Kin* in the gym. Strange it coming up again after previously mentioning the film.

This place is full to bursting just now. The other day we had only biscuits, no bread, at both dinner and tea time. About a hundred had to wait. This morning we had one slice of bread and biscuits and liver. I hope they soon remedy matters.

Since dinner of stew, carrots and potato and some kind of pie and cream, I have washed two hankies, a pair of pants, towel and socks. The laundry arrangements were messed up when we came back from Findhorn and I'm still waiting for the return of dirty washing. I can't do any other than wash a bit for myself.

We are all getting into rows here. I haven't mentioned it before, but I haven't been able to get on with the bloody NCOs and officers. Several of the lads have been on a charge for petty offences, so don't be at all surprised if I get charged in the near future. I kept bursting out in spasms, having told our section commander and a sergeant instructor what I think – all chargeable offences. Tomorrow night at 7 o'clock I have an extra parade for general misbehaviour. So if I get going again I'm liable for CB. They are a lot of inefficient, incompetent, jumped-up, bad-mouthed fools and expect us to run around in circles every time they bark. As I say, we don't do it. It's just too bad really because whatever they do to us shows their inefficiency and lack of control.

Well to continue, my dear, no letter since Wednesday from you. I wrote to Wing in a spare moment last night. Pleased to say I'm doing better with writing up my notes. Our next scheme takes in night and day, four hours on, eight hour off. Always some one working. It is near the coast. Love, N.

30 September 1942

Tuesday after tea

I received your Thursday's letter last night and I'm very happy to note that you are enjoying night work and it's even easier than you expected. Our night scheme is on the box girder bridge. Hope it doesn't pour down with rain. I hope you enjoyed your night out. Do let me know how you got on. In a letter from Mum she was planning what she would like us to do with her. She would like me on her own for a few days! I won't pass any comment on that. Her letter seems an awful lot of blather. Only three more Thursdays – do you hear that! I can hardly contain myself. Loving you, N.

1 October 1942

Thursday NAAFI break

Quite a decent day for a change, with quite a bit of blue sky and sunshine. This morning eighteen of us had to go on the RSM's fatigue party. Not for doing anything wrong, but they said it was a necessity. We finished cleaning the offices out at

9.30 a.m. Later we had talks on town planning and pontooning. It's our half day, but we've had another swimming parade. I suppose I'll do the same as last week with a look round town, tea and pictures and early to bed.

Yesterday we finished heavy bridging and our night scheme on Tuesday was fine and quite warm, though very dark until the moon got up. You mention going into the steel industry – is it nursing or pushing a truck? It's 'outside' once again. They bawl their heads off, but it makes no difference. Off we go.

We now know finally about our leave. It's from October 22 to 31 inclusive, travelling on a Saturday. So only one weekend in that time. Providing you can get time off I'll come straight to you, then Mum and Dad and the lads. Love, N.

A letter to me from N's mother, getting all excited.

Dear Cynthia
I do seem to have a job to write a letter. I wrote to N on Sunday afternoon. I'm running round the village after food, then it's tea and May's dinner and we seem to have food on the go all evening. This afternoon I washed my hair and thought I'd write to you and when I came downstairs Aunt P. was sat here. Of course because I was not going out she was here all afternoon and I got nothing done. It's now 10.15 p.m. May and Pops have gone aloft after a very noisy time and laughing my head off.

May was a paying guest and had severe anaemia. Pops retired usually at 8.30 p.m. and stood on the stairs step indicating he was going to bed. This was always his pattern, trying to catch his wife's eye, as along with Aunty P she was stone deaf. I'll always remember him following Sally, his wife, around the house when he wanted a threepenny bit for his church collection on a Sunday morning. Sally goes on to say, . . .

45

I'm making an attempt once more but can't find notepaper and the room isn't blacked out. Well, I heard from Norman Tuesday. He's ever so good at writing and I *do* love to hear from him. He seems to think he'll be home by the 22nd. Won't it be grand. I bet he's looking forward to it. He's never been away so long before. (Or been so long seeing you, has he?) I expect he'll want to come up and see your people. He will want to see his old pals too. I want him to have a real nice time, and you too of course. N. can have his own bed and if you don't mind sleeping with me, Pops will go to Aunt P. M. has her own room. I've arranged things as best I can. Some home this is when the other two are always sleeping and never a word. I wonder how that pal of his that got hurt up that river is. Haven't they had some awful work, they still need to be fit and well. Can't imagine what he looks like in khaki. I bet he'll soon be in civvies when he gets home. Haven't seen young Wing lately. He's been so good at coming down to see us. He's what I call a gentleman. I know N. thinks a lot of Stan and etc. They are what I call 'rough diamonds' and never appeal to me. I dare say they are good pals.

I've ordered a chicken and if only I could get some more grease I could make hoop-la. Anyhow we'll have a beano. Somehow I've still a bit of flour left and a few eggs for the reunion. We use things as fast as we get them. Affectionately, Ma B.

12 October 1942

Sunday

Back from the battalion exercise in time for dinner and hope to get the afternoon to ourselves. I'm taking this opportunity to write now, as tomorrow until Thursday we will be on the coast doing this scheme. We have weapon slits and trenches to dig and revet, as we call it, and over 3,000 yards of barbed wire fencing to put up. All these are permanent defences and

I understand we are next door to a bombing range and nearly on top of a mine field. So I hope we don't start off in the wrong position. I've already told you about the continual shift working. All we need is good weather, as we have to camp the best way we can.

Your Tuesday's letter came on Thursday along with one from the tax people. (Thought they had forgotten me). I've had further letters from you that must have been held up. I got a parcel from home last night containing a new loaf and butter, tomatoes and apples. May had knitted me a pair of smashing gloves.

Like you I have my dreams. Day-dreaming has become a pastime lately. By the time you get this letter there's only a week to go. I don't know what I'll do tonight. Oh yes I do – Bobby Cameron has gone into our hospital up here for a few days, rest. He hasn't been too well lately, so I'll go up and see him. White beds and clinical smell to remind me of you! All love, N.

15 October 1942

Thursday morning

Back at last and I arn't half thankful. We marched out on Monday morning, as I mentioned, and it was about 9.00 a.m. before we got away, until just after midday and I'll admit it was rough going for about eight miles. We had in excess of the usual marching order: personal washing gear, full water bottle, haversack rations, knife, fork and spoon and all necessary small gear. All these little extra weights tell. After dinner we got down until tea, then a bit more rest and our shift started at 10.00 p.m. until 2.00 a.m. on Tuesday morning. We were wiring in the pitch dark and weren't our hands cut up. I suppose you can imagine what it was like with all the barbs and rolls of it. When we got back, of course still in the dark, we had to find a few blankets, as ours had been taken by the shift we relieved. And so it went on by each shift the whole of the time. We put miles of wire up, built a headquarters dugout and a hell of a lot of weapon slits and yesterday morning, instead of working the usual shifts, we all worked and got finished by 4.00 p.m. We then had tea-cum-dinner and off back at 6.00 p.m. instead of staying the night. All this in a howling rainstorm, arriving about 8.30 p.m. When we had a hot drink, sorted out blankets and got down to it in our own little beds, which before had seemed so hard, but now felt like home sweet home to us. We all slept like logs and instead of being up at 6.30 a.m., not one of us heard a thing until 7.10 a.m. So we just jumped out of bed to breakfast, after which we have been on conservancy. I've managed a wash and shave and feel a bit better. I believe we have bath parade later in the morning.

Since getting back have received your letter and one from your Mum and Dad, one from Wing, one from home and your Saturday's night letter. Wing's was just general news – Can we have a pint together when on leave? Mother says she is getting excited and sort of spring cleaning for my arrival and will have all the flags flying. I'll go along to the office and see if your parcel has arrived. With being away it may be there. I'm sure Mum will find anything in the food line very useful for when she needs it and knowing as I do just how small the rations are.

Have managed a hair cut and my tash trimmed. The lads had started calling me Mustang or Raggy-tash. It had developed so badly the barber had to use shears and comb on it. I am looking more normal so that you will be able to recognise me when we meet. Glorious thought. Will write final details on Sunday. Yours ever, N.

Saturday morning

I've just been writing my last letter home from here and I told them that you would provide some rations, and that you will be telling me when you can get away from Keighley and I'll write my usual Tuesdays.

We spent all of yesterday on revision until 9.30 p.m. and this morning we had the exam and I managed all right. This afternoon I'm going out to celebrate with a pint. I've only had three pints since coming back from Findhorn-in-the-Wilds! Thanks for the offer to nip over to see Mum. She will enjoy that. I don't know what she will say to you offering board money. I guess she will accept.

I got your grand parcel on Thursday night and have devoured all of it and the last of the pears this morning. I'm holding back on some of your marmalade for sandwiches on my way home, as I'm bound to be hungry and may not be able to get much on the journey. Only a few more days now. All love. N.

20 October 1942

Tuesday after dinner

The last communiqué out of Pinefield. Just received your Sunday's letter and noted that what ever happens you will be off for my leave. So happy to know. You will not let any matron, etc., stop you. We live for today from now on.

It's lousy here, pouring with rain and has been since Friday, almost continually. I will be glad to get away from it all tomorrow. We are only messing about finding jobs.

Sunday

Had a few lectures on the Lewis and Vickers machine guns and in the evening had our farewell party in the NAAFI. We had sausage, rissoles and mash, cake and tea in the Soldiers Room for one hour, then into the big room and had an impromptu concert and got merry. The CO came to wish us Godspeed and the officers forgot themselves and sang with high glee and the ranks did their best in the same brand. We cracked up at midnight with our own song - Auld Lang Syne, The King and so to bed.

Yesterday we were on a working party preparing the gym for an ENSA concert which took place last night. It was a smasher, ten artists, all kinds and a lovely soprano who sang amongst many, (for we wouldn't let her go), 'Bonny Mary of Argyle', 'Ave Maria', 'Skye Boat Song', 'Morning Hymn', 'On Wings of Song', Schubert's 'Serenade' and several more. Beautiful they were, dear. She brought the house down. There wasn't a murmer during her singing and that's saying something amongst a few hundred soldiers. There was a long-legged 'It' girl, comedy dancers, magician and another lovely lady whose Christian name was Rodney, who did all the accompanying and gave as a solo 'The Warsaw Concerto' and I loved it.

Today we've been messing about in the rain cleaning up at the lower field works and this afternoon we hand in our rounds, rifles, bayonets etc., get paid, draw our ration cards, and warrants. Had an F.F.I. by the MO yesterday morning and reckon I must be as clean as when I came in. Poor old Bobby Cameron has gone to the hospital at Fort George, so it's unlikely I'll ever see him again, but I have his home address to write to him. I've written to Alice J. who helps our club steward to get the beer lined up and that it will require her at my elbow full-time.

I'll be waiting for you on Saturday – hurry the day. My heart and love. N.

Now I don't remember much about this leave and must have surely managed some time off. Reference somewhere says at times I'd worn green stockings – no tights in those days. N. visited a girlfriend whilst we were together, who was dying of tuberculosis at home. I saw her frail hand waving to me as she lay by the window, the frame of which had been completely removed. She had been exhilarated by N's visit, and wasn't to last very long afterwards.

1 November 1942

Nestfield Dump, Dodsworth Street, Darlington

Here we are once again, but with what a difference! I'd said cheerio to the lads and close friends, got into khaki once more, had tea and said goodbye to Mum and Dad and took the 5.45 p.m. train, which was slow all the way to Selby, caught the connection at York arriving at Darlington at 9.30 p.m. and then my troubles began. Nobody knew of the place. I asked dozens of people until I saw a couple of Red Caps who started to take me but were stopped by one of their sergeants. Once more set off on my search and asked dozens more and after about an hour arrived at Nestfield Dump and the guard room along with others and had to wait until midnight and the storeman coming in from his Saturday night wanderings to get blankets, and retired to rest in the billet, which is an old school taken over by the army. The canteen and cookhouse are in a school in the next street and we had breakfast of cornflakes, some good tea, two rounds of bread, bacon and beans. During the morning an elderly MO looked us over. Later we had an interview with the O.C. and finished by 12.00 p.m. Lunch was roast beef, suet pud, mashed and baked potatoes and cabbage, lovely rice pudding and plenty of it. In fact I sat back feeling I was in Heaven.

It is said that we are having a half day, hanging about until tea time and then try to see the town in the blackout. Our advance party has gone on, apparently, and the new one arrived to take over. It seems we will be moving again within a few days, so do not write to my new address. I mean it, dear. I'm going to miss your letters terribly, but it's no use. Rumour is rife again but I do believe there's a move to Bury St Edmunds in Norfolk. There are fourteen here from Elgin and all the rest, (how many I do not know), are veterans of several years' service. There are three sections, electrical and mechanical workshops and field stores, to which we have to be allocated. So I expect to be in the workshops of my trade, which remains to be seen.

Bailey has arrived from Silsden, Curry from London. Bailey says his little girl didn't know him. Curry's girl is a lovely looking girl if photos are anything to go by.

I broke this letter into four chapters. The fourth is to say how very lovely you made my leave and to thank you, Sweetheart, for you alone. I only wish it could have been twice as long. I hope you didn't find our parting too bad and that you have settled down to work again. I hope that we may be able to stretch and enjoy our thoughts and memories till the next time. Bye, Love. I'll write as soon as possible again. Yours, N.

3 November 1942

Monday

What a surprise and how grand to get your letter so soon! I'm writing to acknowledge and say thanks, it has helped with the gap I've felt being back in harness again after the grand time on leave. Apparently we are not moving yet. A dance has been arranged for Friday night and a football match for Saturday afternoon.

Today I've been on the joinery bench for the first time and I hope I get more of it and less of drilling and the rest. Would you believe it, after all the blancoing we had to do, we now have to scrub our equipment white. We had to parade at 5 for an inspection by the OC. We have to move to other billets, four of us, including Bailey, to our new section about a couple of miles away. Use the address I've already given you. It will find our workshops section. Our army company sign is a black cat arched back, tail up and spitting like hell. It represents Ninth Company – a cat having nine lives! The light has gone out and pen running out, so signing off with the light of my torch. Until next time. Love, N.

5 November 1942

Wednesday night

Still here as expected but our new address is up for future use:
2160917 Spr Bell N
   258 Corps; Field Park Coy. Re
      9th Corps. Home Forces
I suppose this is after we leave here. No other address to be given other than this.

We have been told we are moving for extensive winter training, which can mean a lot of things. This company hasn't seen action for three years, so it will soon be due for some. There's tons of gear of all description, and the Lord knows what. We each carry a six foot rope round our neck for cliff scaling and the O.C. says we will probably be in action in the spring, so don't get the wind up.

A letter has been following me around from Elgin. Wing said there was one on the way from C. Rigby. You will have to excuse delays in my writing you. I've been busy on the bench making fittings and locks for the lorries all week to carry small stock. It's quite like old times. This place is a great big dump near railway sidings and packed with everything you can think of. We have a big pioneer corps of German refugees labouring for us, drivers, mechanical engineers, electricians, welders, labourers and storemen. So you see we can do any job with all the machines of all trades. It's some sight.

On Monday night we went into a club near here for a drink and the locals simply wouldn't let us pay for our drink. Some of the lads have been potato picking these last few days, Bailey and Curry amongst them, and they've each had 8 bob, (40p), a day. Bailey and myself are on fire picket tonight; otherwise we would be seeing *Pardon my Sarong* with Abbott and Costello. We aren't in the wilds like at Elgin. Will you drop Mum a letter when you've the chance? She seems to think the worst about everything. We have a practise 'load up' tomorrow as if ready for off and all in battle order and an inspection. So until next time. Bye and all love. N.

7 November 1942

Friday night

Still here. Thanks for your letter of Wednesday, which I received this dinner time. So refreshing to forget all this for a while. No, I won't keep anything from you. I think we're both able to face facts and know how we stand. Have heard we expect to make Doncaster racecourse for night at the end of the first day and journey's end on the second night somewhere near Bury St Edmunds.

My dear, you have worked wonders with the savings and marvel that you can do so. Don't bother sending me the little odds and ends that I love so and of course the other little titbits that make my eyes sparkle, and the others too. Don't worry about the poorness of your letters, they are wonders of news and love. I look forward to each one with more pleasure, if that is possible, and don't worry that they aren't doing justice to me because they are.

We have been out all day since reveille at 5 a.m. till 6 p.m. tonight, then pay parade and tea. By then it was 7.30 p.m. and have had a clean up and made my bed and sending you these few lines before going for a drink. Bailey is waiting for me on one side and Curry on the other, so if I finish abruptly it's because I'm being man-handled. As I've said, up at 5 a.m., marched to the wagons and camouflaged them, had breakfast at 10.30 a.m., off until midday, then rigged all the machines up – we had a scheme being attacked by other sections. Then we had dinner at 4.00 p.m. and got back as arranged. It's been hectic. Must close. I sense an attack coming on. Until Sunday. All love. N.

10 November 1942

Monday night

Betty sent me this writing paper. Did I tell you that I'd developed into a miniature cook. It's this way. When out on that scheme we won a couple of eggs – well, Curry did, but he managed to smash one in his pocket. I took charge of the other and together with having won some bread, margarine, salt and 6d. ($2\frac{1}{2}$p) worth of chips, I concocted a beautiful dish over the fire in my mess tin. The praise still rings in my ears! Today Bailey has been picking spuds and won two eggs and so we've had more of the above and a bottle of Yorkshire relish and supper is assured once again – I hope. I'll get brayed if I mess it up! Incidentally, Bailey got 11s. (55p), today so we get a drink as well, otherwise we are flat.

We have moved up to our section billets from the school and in a completely new pub. It's never been taken over, a grand place, but cold. There's hot and cold water and wooden ply beds. There's a NAAFI in the bar. All ablutions and any other rooms are sleeping quarters, the cookhouse being just up the road in a big hall where we held the dance on Saturday night. We didn't go.

I was on guard yesterday morning until 8.00 a.m. this morning and have had this afternoon off to make up for it. I've scrubbed my equipment and had a kip. On Saturday morning I slunk off into town for a hair cut and look around. Then I came back for dinner. In the afternoon four of us went to see *Gone With the Wind*. We hadn't much cash and the lowest priced seats were 3s. (15p) and all were full, but the lassie in the office and the attendant put their heads together and let us in the 4s. (20p) ones. Grand of them wasn't it? The picture ran for ten minutes short of four hours and was beautiful. That's the only word I can find to express it. Both Bailey and I were weeping like females at intervals – it's the best film I've ever seen. You must see it at all costs. It's all in technicolour and lots of people come into it during the American Civil War. I'd like you to experience the same pleasure as me; the wondering, the sadness and laughter, the spectacle and beauty of the scenes. A really memorable epic with Vivian Leigh, Leslie Howard, Clark Gable and Olivia De Haviland.

I managed to write to CR and Jessie whilst on guard duty. We met old Bob Bain, a joiner from Leeds, a pal of mine at Elgin last night. He is stationed a few miles away. Amongst some of the things he told us was that five of our lads had gone to Halifax. So it will be embarkation leave and over the waves for them within a week or two. I wonder!

Think I'm about stumped for more but I'll try and draw you 'our cat'. Perhaps you will recognise our corps if you see the sign on a yellow background. That's all. Love, N.

Wednesday night

It's nearly 11.00 p.m. and I'm on borrowed paper and using a borrowed pen from Curry as mine are all packed up for morning. We set off at 9.30 a.m. for Doncaster as I've said before, and aiming for Bury St Edmunds which is in Suffolk. By the way, I'd love a letter for Monday morning. We are skint again. Curry has only $1\frac{1}{2}$d. ($\frac{1}{2}$), Bailey $2\frac{1}{2}$d. (1p) and me $8\frac{1}{2}$d. ($3\frac{1}{2}$p). We feel very browned off. Not much to report and everybody is ready for bed. All love, N.

15 November 1942

Saturday morning

Well, we've arrived safe and sound and rather tired. I received your Tuesday's letter this morning and it's found me all right. Up at 6.00 a.m. on Thursday morning, breakfast at 7.00 a.m. and away by 10.00 a.m. via Thirsk, Northallerton and many places I didn't know, until Doncaster racecourse. That was about 4.00 p.m. We drew two blankets each and had beds in the stands, the whole of which had been taken over by the army. All the railings had been taken down – presumably for scrap. The paddocks and enclosures lined with water tanks, trenches and shelters, and of course the lavatories were just right for the troops, the stand fronts covered in and all the terraced parts covered with beds and palliases on which we slept. The totes are now cookhouses and officers army headquarters. The whole place is solely used for troops on route and convoys. There is a NAAFI here but as we have nowt we toasted over the fire and went to bed at 9.00 p.m. Friday morning we were up at 3.30 a.m., breakfast at 4.15 a.m. and away by 6.00 a.m. A fine day greeted us. We passed through a town about 7.00 a.m. which I believe was

Retford after Bawtry, then Stamford, which was lovely with its old thatched roofs and buildings. Then Gainsborough, Peterborough and lovely Huntingdon, a beautiful Cambridge and you would love Newmarket, the racing town on the edge of the Downs. All cobble streets, market square, rows of trainers stables, some brick – like replicas of small cottages as clean as any house, miles of trees and miles of beech avenues, all changing colour and meeting overhead. A wonderful sight. After Newmarket came this place of which we know very little. It was 4.30 p.m. and soon very dark. We didn't touch Bury St Edmunds and I understand it's about thirty minutes walk away and full of troops and especially Americans and there's queueing for everything – even beer.

Saturday Night at 8.00pm

This is the second attempt since beginning, so hope I'm more successful. I think we had just arrived and allocated huts, those dome-shaped ones called Nissen huts, with beds on two tiers, a stove and best of all a wooden floor. Then tea and after drawing four blankets each, went to bed. It was cold in bed I'll admit, as we hadn't the wherewithal for a fire and no paliasses, but today we have, stuffed with good clean wheat straw and pillow ditto. The stove is now on and red-hot, so we should have a better night. Today has been fine and two of us, (joiners), have been erecting company signs all morning and after dinner, 'notice no half day this week'. We were rigging up one of the machine saws until 4.00 p.m. Then pay parade which we missed yesterday and since tea have done some washing and a good scrub of myself, and lo and behold it was 8.00 p.m. before I'd time to look round – and it's Saturday night.

On our way here we saw umpteen colossal airdromes and American army Air Corps personnel and dozens of those little 'jeeps' you may have seen on T.V. darting about the countryside. Saw lots of pheasant in groups and small deer. This camp is huge, in fact a park and dozens of trees, some hundreds of years old: oak, beech, elm and lime. Under these are all the Nissen huts and forming a huge canopy are these lovely trees. A great rambling house up in the dim distance is the officers' quarters.

Have already had two letters from you. You make no reference to leaving your job. I've not made any mention of moving about to Mum and Dad so that they don't get the wind up. In fact I say very little. It's gone 9.00 p.m. and I have to write home. All love, N.

17 November 1942

Monday night

Bury St Edmunds

No letter today and I had so looked forward to one. Never mind, there could be two tomorrow. Yesterday was a cold but sunny one, starting with rifle inspection, then unloading stores until dinner time and half day off. Bailey, Curry and I had a shower and did some washing. Then I mended two pairs of socks and sewed three buttons on my greatcoat, only to find that one pinged off when put on. This took until teatime.

All the hut went out for the evening. I'm almost skint. I resolved never to be that way again. Bailey and Curry played hell with me. Curry had a 10s. (50p) postal order. I just could not go into town with them with only two bob and look around and sponge on Curry. Instead I got my battle order ready for today and cleaned my rifle and boots. For the first time whilst in the Forces I did a spot of reading. Having kept the stove going I made some toast. A funny thing happened. The butter was wrapped in a letter from Bailey's wife and having spotted the name 'Bell' I couldn't help reading it. It said, 'Is Bell's girl still at Keighley? If so, she could come and see me and I'll smile when I do see her as I seem to know such a lot about the pair.' I wonder what she means.

Today we've been out on so-called 'extensive training', like the infantry training at Elgin – rushing about and marching eight miles. It's hard work! We had dinner under a sweet chestnut tree and brought lots of nuts back and cooked them on the stove. They are a little smaller than the bought ones. It has been a grand day, lovely country, marvellous trees with hedges of lilac.

19 November 1942

Wednesday night

It's been a lovely day but very cold. Been out on demolitions and musketry, felling trees with explosives and doubling, laying and charging through down land set with little pine trees. Firing away and very hard work. My primitive instincts didn't mind it; the bugbear is the cleaning of equipment afterwards, but I've got that done and I'll be in bed once I've written to you. I've had your birthday greeting and also from Mum and Dad. You've no idea how I look forward to your letters. Mother says she feels miserable at my departure to the unknown. Many thanks for the stamps but don't send any more or anything else at this point of uncertainty. I'm happy that you are enjoying some social activity away from routine.

Yes, the Bells all rang and it sounded good. Wish it had been the 'all clear.' Can't imagine when it will be over and I've a feeling we shall see foreign service. We haven't heard anything and although I think we have a definite victory in Africa I'm much in the dark about the other spheres – but I'm confident of success. Bye for now, dear. N.

Sunday after dinner

Quite a decent autumn day, cold but fine, though it rained a little last night whilst in Bury. The first time out on pleasure bent, so to speak. We walked there, three of us, and another joiner younger than me who has been in since the beginning. Quite a nice fellow, courting a Darlington girl, and is he in love! Bury is a lovely old world town. You would love it. Rather rambling, with little small paned windows, even in the shops, some thatched roofs and plenty of half-timbering. In fact I'd expected to see at any moment a coach and horses galloping along, powdered wigs and crinolines. It was 4.00 p.m. and teatime so we went along to what is known as the Athenia Club for tea. This is actually an authors' club taken over by the forces. It is a lovely place, something like a Masonic club I should imagine. A large hall with a stage at one end, a pillared side recess from which refreshments were served. Its all very stately, a high domed roof, plush curtains and a most perfect sweep on the staircase up to the reading room and writing room. This had a coke fire, plenty of tables and chairs and is lined with shelves of books of all kinds and gilt notices up all over saying 'silence'. We had two cups of tea, three sandwiches and two buns for a few coppers. We then had a sedate boozing time and then to the Salvation Army hostel for sausage and beans and bread and butter for 8d. ($3\frac{1}{2}$p). We then caught the 'liberty' truck and to bed at 10.30 p.m. By the way, in the afternoon we had a football match. Workshops versus motor transport, me playing right fullback and got kicked behind the ear. I heard that someone had remarked that that 'old man with the tash' seemed a good player, so help me. We were losing 2-0 when the ball burst and the match abandoned. We hope to trounce them in the replay. I've been at work most of the week and have to work this afternoon on the Chief Royal Engineer's wireless van. It's a rush job and I'm expecting to get my half day later this week.

After tea

It's about time you were thanked for your birthday present. So much appreciated and many thanks. Mother thinks I'm starving and sent a parcel with a small cake, pork pie, honey, butter, cheese, apple pastry and a dozen apples. I got several family cards – so didn't do too bad. I've told Bailey that you would like to meet his wife whilst at Keighley and he is to make known to her and arrangements made. He is to go on a course of signalling at Catterick for about a month or so. All love until Tuesday. N.

25 November 1942

Tuesday night

It's foggy and trying to rain but the old stove is roaring away and all's well with the world. Two of us had our half day yesterday as expected and went into Bury for tea at the YMCA and the pictures and got a lift back to camp with one of the trucks. My mate retired to the reading and writing room. I wrote a line or two to your mum and dad but didn't think I'd done them justice, but I knew they would be pleased to hear from me. The company is moving off tomorrow to fresh fields. Being in the rear party, we don't go until Thursday. I'm blowed if I know where. But more than thirty miles from Thetford and north of here and don't think we will be long there either. Rumour says Reading and the Lord only knows where else but I'll let you know of change of address. Carry on writing as usual and trust to them being forwarded. I couldn't stand another week without hearing from you – the miles apart and bounding waves don't bear thinking of, and it will surely come. I must write to Jessie whose birthday is a week after mine and also write home. As always, N.

Thursday Night   **Thetford**

I hope to get quite a bit written but in case not it's because we are on a scheme at 7.00 p.m., which I believe lasts until early morning. Defending some static water or something but more about that another time, if I get the chance and however little I get said I hope for you to get it by the weekend. The post comes here by duty truck twice a day. Your mail will find me just the same. We have moved on now about twenty miles in a big wood in wooden huts and wooden beds with four blankets – I've managed to get five. There's also a small stove. We are only here until Tuesday when we move on to East Harling. I'm blowed where next. Times are a bit hectic and I'm sorry to be so brief. I've had a letter from home and yours of Tuesday which I had been so longing for. Once again I'm waiting for pay day and have sent 10s. (50p) home for insurance. As always, N.

30 November 1942

Sunday Night   **Rigglesworth Camp**

It's raining, I don't know what time it is and we are up to the ankles in mud, but the old stove is going. It's been our half day and we have had a smashing dinner and tea and all things told, I'm not so bad. Thursday night we had the scheme I told you of but it only lasted to about 11.00 p.m. It rained buckets and we were laid out in it and charging over rough downland defending against the other company, who have gone today. Our section under a sergeant were all wiped out but two of us who lay doggo and in turn wiped out the rest of the enemy. So we didn't do bad.

It rained all Friday and we were on works in the morning, drill in the afternoon and pay parade. Saturday morning I was on works again. In the afternoon I was picked for the intersectional match, playing right full back. I now am as stiff as a corpse and have a kicked ankle. We lost 2–1, yet a good game. I shook the CSM up quite a bit, so squaring accounts. In the evening I wrote the Chester folk and Mrs H. thanking them for parcel and 10s. (50p) note. We went to the NAAFI until 9.00 p.m., where three of our lads were on the piano, drums and sax and good too, but it was so cold. This morning we had a later Sunday reveille and church parade and inspection. To the NAAFI, rifle inspection, dinner and finished for the day. So this afternoon been to bed, had my tea of pressed meat, beetroot and bread and scrape. Tomorrow we start with a later parade at 8.30 a.m. Had your Thursday's letter yesterday which along with others, are coming from the Bury camp. We move on Wednesday. As a point of interest, we have a new cook (army catering company) who has had his embarkation leave prior to joining us. I could of course get a leave early in the New Year, which will mean you trying to be off the same time. You must see what you can do. I couldn't bear it otherwise. We have a section sergeant who is responsible for law and order to each section and a staff sergeant responsible for the work we do. Our 'staff' as we call him, informed me yesterday that he has forwarded my name to the OC for regrading and trade pay, as we are up to strength in the carpenters and joiners and will have to wait for a vacancy and may get back pay when on strength. The Lord knows when that will be and although I could apply for reposting, I want to stay with the lads I know. It's a good mob to be in. Isn't it time that the chickens are taken off our plot as per the buying contract? Signing off now until Tuesday. All love, N.

Tuesday night

Today was very dull and we had quite a heavy rainstorm. I've been on works all day on a blackout screen, a posting box for outside the company office and making a new 'bridge' for a string bass for the dance band. Yesterday was on works all day too. I managed a haircut and wrote to Wing in the evening. I've sewn all the buttons on my greatcoat, so was quite busy. On Saturday after writing to you, I went into the NAAFI and found Joe Davidson a Newcastle laddy who was at Elgin with us and had just come in with 558 Field Coy. I'm a bit stumped for something to say as I haven't heard from you since Saturday, but I'm not surprised as Monday's post has got lost somewhere and they have been hunting for it all over. They will turn up sometime, but I'd rather have them now.

We have only been here six days but all are fed up. It's absolutely black, while early morning when the moon comes out and with all the trees it's worse still. There are weapon slits dug all over the place and although I've yet to go down one, most of the members of this hut have. I've been lost nearly every time I've gone out to the extent of finding the place I've wanted to go to and as the ablutions are about 200 yards away it's quite a job going for a wash. In fact we go in convoy. The wcs are the best we've struck yet. Six big pans in two rows, a bit of wood over them and a yard strip of sacking about eighteen inches from the ground around them. But as we have to tinkle there, the wood is always wet and the sacking gets stamped down in the darkness. So that it's a very funny sight to see a row of blokes with bottoms in the air and belts round neck! It's hard luck when I have to write about that to you, dear, but think you will see the funny side of it. Must away. Always yours, N.

4 December 1942

Thetford

It's Saturday night and we are off for Wallingford in the morning about 140 miles away, I believe, on the upper reaches of the Thames. Lord only knows what will happen about our mail and the parcel you are sending.

9 December 1942

Tuesday   **Wallingford**

We set off in the dark on Sunday morning, passing through Thetford, Newmarket again and Mildenhall with its colossal aerodrome from which the Kings Cup air races used to start in peace time. After that Luton, a large industrial town where they make hats, amongst other things. The streets here were lined with oil burners for creating artificial fog as a screen against enemy planes. Then Harlow with another big aerodrome. It seems all aerodromes, doesn't it, but then it was so. Hitchin came next, I think only twenty five miles from London. Here we turned more west and passed Aylesbury and Princes Risborough and finally Wallingford. It's a lovely place, of what little I've seen of it. It's situated on the Thames. Real old world with some beautiful period houses and looks very prosperous. After travelling all day last Sunday on a cheese sandwich and no drink, our one and only meal couldn't be got ready until 8.00 p.m. – understandable under the circumstances. We dashed out to find something for the inner man and behold, we found a grand WVS canteen nearly opposite our billets and it's from there I am writing you now. Two wooden huts joined together with toilets, baths and hand bowls, just off the entrance a long bar which served the food. Plenty of seating and tables, many games, wireless and piano.

66

There are WAAFS and RAF in strength. Anyhow we had some very good food and actually some egg sandwiches, the first I'd seen.

11 December 1942

Thursday night

Still at Wallingford and another rushed letter, I'm afraid. We have an extra parade awarded because of dirty rifles. It seems very paltry to me to do this thing because of a bit of dust, when we have been doing hard and heavy work from dawn till dusk all the week. We can't do anything about it so it will be two hours' cleaning up and a parade at 8.30 p.m. in order to spoil an evening and the old man is sure to be late. We have been busy on the old Thames again, pontooning and cutter racing, so I'm just about a physical wreck. But if anything, one can say it's good for a change. We have swans as companions and today saw my first black swan. I cannot get over it. Somehow I thought black swans were mythical or only the names of pubs. Also several ducks flew over us whilst up river and I've come across the most divine place. I wish you could have seen it – a tumbling stream joining the river like a waterfall and at the little backwater it formed was a half timbered boathouse with a lovely motor launch and a view of an old stately house, with wide lawns and beech trees and matured gardens.

I wrote to Betty and Ted last night and tried to sound interesting. Jessie wrote but I can't understand it, the writing is so small. Haven't heard from you since last Saturday. Longing for your letters. Bye, N.

Sunday night   **East Harling**

I'm back at last and found your parcel and two letters. Thank you very much. So please excuse a lapse in writing and short letters at the moment. I'm dead tired and it is late – and I do deeply appreciate hearing from you as it's the answer to prayer. You do know I love everything you send – just give me time. I'll just mention that we came back the same way as we went and outside Luton a great big new hospital, the type you dream about in the shape of an 'H', flat topped and rustic bricked, all square angles and balconies jutting out for all the world as if no support. We arrived back here at dusk and everything to clean up. So until Tuesday. All love, N.

Monday night   **East Harling**

It seems we will be here for a bit. The OC said today that we may be going to Wallingford for a few weeks.

I have sampled the parcel you sent and shared the pastry. I'm using the jam and where did you get this grand dripping from? I've started on the nice shaving cream and the stick-on labels are now in use. In fact everything's being used and thank you so very much.

It looks as if I'll have to catch up on a bit more writing as it's in the air for me to take an NCO course. Well it's something, but with the threat of embarkation makes me wonder. Every small opportunity I will write you. We are under a lot of heavy duty filling in long days. Love, N.

Thursday dinner

Had your Sunday's twelve page letter on matrimony last night, dear, but won't be answering just now as I haven't much time and eight different people to write to in answer to theirs. I'm up to my neck with the NCO's course and doubling all day long and lectures at night. We have rigid inspections by the OC every morning, necessitating hours of scrubbing at day's end. Then bed, glorious bed! Love, N.

20 December 1942

Sunday afternoon at home

Do hope you got my wire and understand it. Yes I'm at home – yes really. Don't upset yourself, it's fourteen days embarkation leave. We were awakened yesterday morning at 1.30 a.m. and notified of it in order for the clerks to get all our tickets and passes made out, which they were doing all night. We were eventually paid and left by truck after dinner for Thetford. Leaving Thetford at 3.30 p.m., we changed at March and via Peterborough, Grantham, Retford and Doncaster. Changing there I caught our old 7.05 p.m. from Sheffield and arrived here about 10.00 p.m.

As you would expect, I've been out seeing my close friends and will be up at the club for you to ring me in the evening, as I mentioned in the wire. Thought it better this way, as by the time you were located it could have taken ages.

First and foremost, although I may not go abroad for sometime, I may have to go straight away. So this is perhaps the best chance we may have. On my waking hours I have thought and thought and better thought and here follows what I think would be the most sensible course of action. If I can make arrangements for the wedding to take place just after Christmas this would give you more time to do what you have to do. Let me know what you decide – it's your choice and I'll fit in. If it's to be at this end I'll approach the Reverend – and I'm stumped for the short honeymoon. There are several things to consider in so short a time about putting our folks up either your end or mine. Whatever pleases you. I'll wait for your ring and letters. Until tonight. All love, N.

The matron at the hospital where I was nursing was a most attractive and beautiful person. She must have been chosen on this account but it belied her make up. I went to her office as duty directs, explaining my position and asked for time off for my 'occasion' and knowing this was allowable during wartime conditions by the authorities. 'You can contact Head Office, but not from this hospital and I'm not ringing up for you.' Lovely woman – no wartime camaraderie here – a very ascetic person. I waited a few days for permission coming through via her office, after using an outside phone to the authority the same day in off-duty time, when she had been so cold and in an unremitting attitude. Meanwhile, packing up all my personal things and just when it was imperative and a time factor, I was ready to go – this was by hook or by crook. I did have one friend who took some luggage to send on to me and, knowing the situation, rushed into my room and pushed me in the wardrobe and said 'Shush!' and disappeared only just in time as someone came yelling down the corridor and into my room for me. I gave no response and was away as soon as the coast was clear. I did write to the authority and explain and because of the situation prevailing, asked for my release from the the Civil Nursing Service for future duty towards my husband.

Deeds are best, be it great ones or small. To act well by others is noblest of all. After over fifty years I'm still in touch with the friend who helped me escape.

And so the simplest and quietest wedding took place on 28th December 1942 at 9.00 a.m. by special licence from York. No photography and the best we could do of a wedding breakfast in N. 's home and village. I'd worn a black and green costume and black mantilla-like hat, hardly glamorous. Only immediate members of each family were present and we were off in the afternoon to stay a couple of days with my brother and sister-in-law. We were to have a meat and potato pie for supper. Hours and hours went by and still the pie wasn't ready or even the crust put on. Being so tired I could hardly keep my eyes from crossing. Being polite we waited and hung on. Do you know what it's like being punished for something you hadn't done? My brother and sister-in-law seemed so bright and merry and pleased with themselves, I'd rather have had an apple-pie bed.

8 January 1943

Sunday night   **East Harling**

How's the wife?

Which reminds me of a couple of men meeting in the pub.
1st man: 'Where's the wife tonight?'
2nd man: 'I've left her at home in bed.'
1st man: 'Why, is she badly?'
2nd man: 'No, she's only dead.'

When I got back here there was a little pile of Christmas mail. A pair of lovely knitted socks from cousin Edith. A letter-card from you and your letter and present – bless your heart. I'd thought of sending a £1 back, as I scrounged a £1 from you; instead I'm putting it on one side for a rainy day. I've just been to see the clerk about your married allowance. The certificate will be sent to your home with the allowance. The allotment, as far as I can gather, with my compulsory

71

stoppage, is about 32s. (£1.60), as I only get 17s. 6d. (87½p). I hope you don't mind me not making a voluntary allowance.

Will you tell Mum and Dad of my movements? It will relieve their feelings as time is the factor at the moment.

The journey to Doncaster was perishing but I managed a coffee and there was a fire in the waiting room. I met a girl I knew when I worked at Lockings and we travelled together until Lincoln. We were an hour late when we got into Thetford. There were eight of us and on ringing up, the duty wagon was at Norwich fetching lads back from there and would we find somewhere to kip. After walking about until about 11.00 p.m. we found a REME camp who started to put us up for the night. We had just got a bed each in an empty hut, no blankets, when the duty truck found us after all and took us back to camp, arriving cold and very weary. My grand mates had made our beds up and all our kit ready and had kept a whopping fire. Wasn't it grand of them? No sooner in bed then up as usual and a full day on works, altering the CRE's wireless wagon and now tonight on guard. I musn't grumble, it's the first I've done since Darlington. Alas, it was freezing. The lads have had to remove their 'cap badge'. We have a new sergeant and several rankers. Haven't any news of further movement. Some lads who had only had seven days have gone off for their other seven. We are busy making packing cases and frames. It looks as if the CADRE class has gone west and work started again. Not that I mind that, as it wouldn't be nice crawling about in the snow and ice. Well now, I'll write solely to you again, dear. Thanks for making my leave so grand and for doing the things that make life seem more normal. Think now of all the happy times we've had and I'm always with you. Bailey is on leave and must have been here as his kit is in our hut. Curry is browned off as usual but going with another half dozen on detachment tomorrow, maybe for a couple of days or months. I'm now going to try to get an hour before I'm on the gate at 11.00 p.m. Take care. Love, N.

Tuesday night

What have you made out about your next move and will you go into industry now that you propose to work from your mum's? My prayers are in my thoughts which I always go through every night before I fall asleep.

No further news of movement except that our sections are to be called platoons. I'm still getting charge of jobs with other carpenters and joiners and I a lonely pioneer – funny isn't it. Still, I expect to get trade pay eventually.

The others have been getting washed, now it's my turn. Remember me to my mum and dad as you pass news along to them. N.

13 January 1943

Friday night

Half days seem a rarity lately. Will you do me a favour and look out for either a pocket or wrist watch and I'm not expecting you to pay for one. We are beat for time keeping as our billet corporal is away with Curry and it falls on me to wake the huts etc, as no one bothers. I'm not worried about them, but I've got a job to get up each morning – not knowing the time. It was 7.50 a.m. when we turned out this morning, so of course got no breakfast. Not even a drink. There was a severe frost last night and slight snow. Everywhere is hard and slippery. I've seen the first new moon of the year. At pay parade this afternoon I drew the magnificent sum of 17s. only, (85p). Even shillings are paid out.

Sunday night

After a full day's work and another half day lost.

The wagon took us into Norwich last evening, arriving at dusk. I noticed an awful lot of bomb damage; not as much as Hull perhaps. Overhead a balloon barrage. It seemed otherwise a nice city with fine buildings and wide streets. We alighted at a park. The first four canteens were packed out and we were ready for a hot cup of tea. We found a United Services place in a disused church with a great high roof and stone pillars and an organ. In fact everything except the pulpit and seats. After trying three picture houses we managed one and came out at 9.30 p.m. when we had three half-pints until 10.00 p.m. No military vehicles are allowed in the city after 10.30 p.m. We waited as long as we could for two lads and finally had to go without them. They arrived back about 3.00 a.m. after walking most of the twenty five mile journey. Another truck load had gone at 2.30 p.m. on their half day. They lost their way and finished at Lowestoft, then at Ipswich and got back just after the two lads who had walked.

No movement news and have dozens of crates to make for machinery, etc. Only two letters from you since I came back and it seems ages ago. Take care. All love. N.

From now on I had to get used to this craving for letters – always sent as regularly as previously arranged – receiving no fault on either side. Delays were no fault of sender.

Your last letters arrived quickly. Enclosed in this letter is my medical card for you to save and a letter from Bailey's wee daughter. Bailey says they have received the wedding cake and expecting you back at the hospital, were going up to see you and I'll tell you in my next letter what sort of reception they had. By the way, I've started my old pipe tonight for the first time. It affords no end of amusement with the lads. They have already threatened to shave half my tash off!

Knowing that you plan to spend monthly weekends with Mum and Dad, Mum says you have told her that if my expected letters don't arrive on time, you don't feel like getting up. Although I am far from brave, I can face the future after the war with a much better face and ease of mind. Just to think that I was amongst the lads in this lot and shared their lot too. Somehow, however much one does at home it doesn't compare to the actual job here – the high spirits and comradeship, then at times pettiness and boredom. But at the bottom of us we can and do realise the strength of each other and think as I say perhaps not rightly, but we are in it and away from freedom, home comforts and all things we cherish most and little cash.

Our snow has all gone with rain taking over and everywhere water and mud. Mother says she was awake all Friday night worrying, thinking that I'd gone. It must be rotten for her, bless her. But I wish she wouldn't worry her old head. Somehow I can't talk to her in the same way I do to you. She asks if we have sent cake to the Chester folk. So will you?

We've had a complete check-up for overseas. Battle order inspection and arms drill, aircraft recognition, lecture by the OC on the war situation and our probable movement. He thinks it will be North Africa, as we do. We've just no idea. We still seem to have plenty of essential work at hand. Will be with you again soon. N.

15 January 1943

Thursday night

I'm very pleased you had a good day out at the Leeds pantomime. Mum says it was good too, but was unable to hear. Yet it was a change. I have been able to get you some dress material and will be sending it on – seeing as you are a dab-hand with a machine. Let me know if if appeals to you.

Yes, I have been pulling your leg! It's just that I like to know what you are doing. It's the interest I have in you. Yesterday was lousy and missed PT, of which I'm very fond. It tones me up for the day. Thanks for the stamps. Right on time and very much appreciated. I've found something I want and that's darning needles. Can't seem to get any here and if you can manage some MacLeans toothpaste. We have been on works and finished with a lecture by the OC on the first field dressings, artificial respiration and hygiene. All of course in order for our travels abroad. Today works again and the OC on identification of Germans and Americans, who presumably we shall meet on our travels. I've been detailed for work straight away to finish off an LCV which is a local communication vehicle – a wireless van etc., made up from a two ton truck.

Heavy rain has stopped us from a twenty five mile march – and I hope it does the same tomorrow. Just come back from the NAAFI and had full supper for a tanner. All love, N.

Our rapturous love was in all letters exchanged and ours to cherish during stressful times of parting – omitted now in this narrative – yet I may break loose at times.

18 January 1943

Sunday night

What am I going to say about your watch, your letters and your pork pie? Not having any idea, not the faintest, of what would be in the parcel, I found your precious watch. I didn't know what to do. I believe I nearly cried and almost sent it back. Instead thank you so very much. It's in my inside pocket during the day and at night on a rail above my head. A beautiful thought that prompted you to send it.

Six of us immediately set about the pie and the lads said it was like being at home and I endorse the remarks. Have been playing football this afternoon, me at left half full back and for a change won 5-3. Two showers later and I'm very tired. Two FFIs (free from infection), in a week. They aren't half keen.

Bailey came back on Wednesday and brought us a present. I'm sending it on to you and I know you would like to thank his wife. I'm not letting on to you what it is so that you enjoy the surprise. Feeling all in and ready to flop into bed. Route march tomorrow. All love, N.

22 January 1943

Thursday night

Haven't had a letter from you since Tuesday and cannot find much to say. We have a rush of work and another LCV truck to start on along with normal work. It's possible we will miss out on half days. Many rumours fly around almost half hourly. We call them 'pigeons'. Being rumours, I don't repeat them. Some say North Africa and others any part of the globe. I'll close again, my dear, not having done you justice. All my love. N.

There's been a gale blowing all day and now since tea pouring with rain. Playing football again against 242 company we won 3-1. Yesterday afternoon the 9th Corp REs were playing the 11th Armoured Division at Rugby in Cambridge. Some of our lads were in the team. Two wagonloads were allowed to go. We set off late and arrived late and as we drew up at the park it started to rain and hail and a right old gale. So went and had some food and then went to the pictures. We saw Noel Coward's *In Which We Serve* and it really grips you from start to finish. A straightforward story of a ship and men, with gems of actors. Do try and see it if you can and please don't cry too much. There was a Donald Duck cartoon and Pathetone News. From there we went to a WVS canteen and had supper and then a couple of pints, returning 'home' at 10.30 p.m. to arrive at midnight. Cambridge was quite a big place with several colleges and prefects in mortar boards and gowns.

We've had a security lecture by the security guards – a branch of the army. All about keeping 'mum' and not divulging information or communicating in any way with anyone once leaving port of embarkation. So won't be able to let you know my whereabouts.

I've finished all my stock of news. Our kit deficiencies are being made up and everything getting steadily nearer completion. There are conferences being held daily and anything can happen. I do hope I see you again before we sail, but don't bank on it, but a couple of days would be grand. Until next time. Bye love, N.

27 January 1943

You will have started your new job by now in the medical department of your steelworks and I'm wondering how it goes with you and how the shift hours will work. I wish you luck and hope you will enjoy it. The material I mentioned is on its way to you. The girl in the office at the hospital said you had gone off to marry 'Captain Bell'. I wouldn't think you would say that or Bailey is pulling my leg.

News from Mum says the postman has had another fall and cracked a rib. Cousin John from Brough has gone overseas. She also says she has been into town to spend her Christmas boxes and got some stuff for a night gown and a stew-jar so that you can have yours back! Mum is getting a supplementary pension to make up the cash equivalent of my late donation. Hull was bombed again on Friday night with sulphurus bombs. But three planes were shot down. In closing Mum says she hasn't heard from you lately and sends her love.

Still busy on works straight away each morning and missing my PT. Always yours. N.

After tea, Tuesday

The weather's not too good today, but certainly better than yesterday when out doing the old cross-country, crawling, marching and running, etc., and attacking enemy positions until dinner. After that we were taken out and dropped as enemy paratroopers (seven of us) and we had to make our way back and take our positions in East Harling. I'm sorry to say we were taken prisoners before we succeeded. The worst of our troubles was to get back for tea, which we did by 5.00 p.m. It had poured down and within ten minutes we were soaked to the skin and quite miserable and fed up. After a decent tea and good hot wash, a cig and round the hot stove felt so much better. Today's weather a bit better and after PT had lectures on booby-traps until dinner, after which the sergeant picked the first six he saw for cleaning up the messy latrines and urinals as the MO was to have an inspection. It wasn't a job I'd have picked myself, it certainly did stink but we finished by 3.00 p.m. and I played football until 4.00 p.m. Had a good hot shower, tea of chips, brawn, pickled cabbage and bread. We have now been married one month and a day. Got your Sunday's letter, darning needles and toothpaste. Wish I could put buttons on for keeps. There's six to go, gloves to darn – never a spare moment. On the open range all day tomorrow. Yours always, N.

Tuesday dinner

This is certainly my Tuesday's letter! I'm trying to catch the 5.00 p.m. post. It's good news. Yesterday half the MT drivers went on forty eight hour leave. Today forty per cent of the whole company are going; the rest of us will go when they come back. I may be able to write you or failing that, send a wire. In any case I will just come to you making the best way I can once the train gets in at Sheffield. It means only a one night stay. I very much doubt if you will be able to get time off at so short a notice. All I can say in closing is that it seems pretty definite and I'm longing for our few short hours together. Now off to some more work. All love, N.

At this late point it should be mentioned that the only method of dating of these letters was by the franking of the postal service and so the dates are often later than the written letters. In some instances – not many – the date was not legible on the stick-on labels of the envelopes and so a bit of judgement in the order of continuity falls somewhat haphazard.

And so in the middle of the night I heard a loud whistling which must have wakened more than me. Even today I remember being amused. How Norman could have been so joyful after walking twelve miles from the railway station was quite amazing. In a very short time I was seeing him off at the station, feeling quite numb.

Monday after tea

Back once again and thanks for the letter waiting for me to read when I got in and to help me over the night. We had a lovely time and lucky that you had time off – but now the long parting. Our advance party goes after the 10th and my address as I've already told you. I'll be writing to you again and continue to do so whilst I can. Once on the move and boarding ship is another thing. Wednesday night and no letter from you or home so presume you think I've moved. Yesterday we didn't do much at all, a route march in the morning and football in the afternoon, in the evening a brains trust session, the rest of the evening trying to squash in all my kit. This morning we have had a further period of cleaning out billets thoroughly and at 11.00 a.m. we had to parade fully dressed with kit as for movement. In fact we didn't know if the hour had arrived until we had been dismissed for dinner. After dinner we did a bit more cleaning up outside the billets and then were paid for last week and this week. Tomorrow's orders are up and I see we are confined to barracks after 4.00 p.m. – a move could come any time. I hope you will be all right and manage to keep smiling as I love to see you. As always, N.

2160917 Sapper BELL N
258 CORP FLD PK COY RE
C/O APO4660
LONDON

Official Paid Letter   **Undated**

Well at last we are aboard and that's about all I can say. I cannot tell you anything, but I do want you to know how I'm faring. We have been supplied with a green envelope in which we can place up to three complete letters. I'm writing you and Mum and Dad. My contribution is two. Notify each other should any letters get lost in transit. A censor will score out anything doubtful – even the date. So I am proposing numbering each of my letters to you – this being No. 1.

I'm awfully sorry, dear, but it has dawned on me that it is your birthday today and as usual I have forgotten it. I hope you will excuse me as we have been rushing about a bit lately and to be honest I did forget it, though I'd remembered previously. Going away on your blinking birthday. I hope to be back by your next one.

We had travelled all night, starting after dark and arriving here before daylight at a place we had never dreamed of. I'm afraid I cannot describe the ship for obvious reasons, but it's exactly like the ships I've worked on. We are quite a mixed bag and still filling up and no idea of the sailing time or destination. Another thing, dear, I don't know if you will get further mail from me for some time. I've no doubt it will be some time before getting any from you. I have had your letter of Tuesday before we set off and since getting back off leave.

Thanks for your good wishes. I know I'll always have them. I'll be thinking of you – in fact I seldom think of anything else. Must close, my love, and if it's not too late – a 'Very Happy Birthday' and all my love, N.

Green letter on board (Second letter)   **Active Service**

The first day on board I wrote you. We didn't do much but get settled in and sampled our first shipboard meals. Plenty of it but didn't enjoy them a great deal – they had a peculiar taste. We retired at the early hour of 9.00 p.m. and were soon asleep. On the second day all but four of us were on boat-drill, etc. The other four were on guard duty for twenty four hours on a prisoner in the cells. All normal police duties are carried out as on shore. On the third day, after coming off guard we have done nothing but dinner and watched the coast recede – away behind us – in the distance home and you. I wonder how long. Meals are improving. Mutton disguised in many ways but now we've had pork, cabbage and mash and a beautiful pudding of the Christmas type, full of peel and fruit – really delicious. There is also a canteen, but a day one. No beer served at all. We can buy almost everything, all appearing to be Argentine products – great tins of peaches, pears and like for 11d. ($4\frac{1}{2}$). All kinds of chocolate at 3d. (1p) a bar. Biscuits too. Apart from the fact that probably some won't be able to eat a deal soon for some time. We should be OK.

I'd like to tell you of all the ships we have passed and the others on board but it is impossible. I'm going to miss you like Hell, but will kid myself that I won't. Happy memories. Norman.

Examiner 1843 passed.

26 March 1943

Air Mail Letter $3\frac{1}{2}$d. Stamp

I have to have this in the post by 8.30, so writing to say that my previous letter may take about three weeks, whilst this type of letter by airmail will get to you sooner. You can get this type of letter at your post office with a 6d. ($2\frac{1}{2}$p) stamp to send me by return. I cannot get more than one a week of this type of letter – so if I keep sending to you, will you pass on to Mum and Dad any normal news as soon as possible? I'm still alive and kicking. For your ears only, we had a bit of a scramble at the end of the trip. Anyway I'm fine apart from aches and pains and blistered feet. The company is in a big farmhouse; all around us vine and olive fields. Date, fig, orange and lemon orchards all out of bounds to us. Of course understandable.

I know you will have been writing me and I'm looking forward to the post catching us up. We are, by the way, in North Africa, having landed out of the Mediterranean and are about 100 miles behind the front and awaiting our transport. I'm thinking of you. Keep smiling. As ever, Norman.

Air Graph

I haven't much time or the inclination to write. Coming up we had the most beautiful country to cross and the Atlas mountains thousands of feet up. Then the world's worst, scrub, cacti and sand. Miles of trackless waste – yes, the desert, and now we are camped with scrubby trees and cacti all around us. Flies by the millions, I've spent most of the day attending to bites and stings and there are some funny sights, me included. We had our first aftermath of battle, and though we are driving ahead rapidly, I'm afraid I was rather awed and a little repulsed by it. The place in ruins, graves, equipment and ammunition littered all over. Needless to say, prisoners coming back and troops and tanks going up all day and night. That's all, dear. Keep our dreams going. All love, N.

25 March 1943

APO (Army Post Office) Fifth Letter

We arrived in port North Africa after an eventful night and what a sight awaited us!

The dock, as you can imagine, was a hive of industry. Native Arabs in tatty clothes everywhere, begging, peddling and scrounging and jabbering away. We marched out here with full pack for about twenty miles – it seemed like 120 – to this place – a large house, not a farm as we know it. Arabs in swarms from the new-born to centenarians. Oxen-drawn carts, mules and all the pomp and custom of centuries ago – ironically there was electric light. At the moment I am sitting at the foot of a whopping date palm, the fruit hanging in clusters about four foot long. There must be hundreds in each.

I am just eating my third orange of the day, which reminds me, we can send an occasional parcel home.

Before leaving the boat we had to hand in our English cash in exchange for every £1, Fr. 200. We are to have an issue of air mail letters and it's possible you will get one before this, so I'm bound to repeat myself. It's the queerest country. The women work all day in the fields and most of the men just sit about. There doesn't seem to be any birth control practised at all; rather the reverse, if anything, and that goes for the fowl life. I've found the queerest-looking things here, chickens in body but with head and neck of a turkey. But there are turkeys knocking around so surmise one must have run amok once in the dim past!

This is a half day for doing our washing. I'm at the bottom of the list so I'm able to write you whilst waiting. Water is a big consideration out here. These days our washing water is from the Arabs' well and unfit for drinking. A guard is stationed by the drinking water, which is purified before delivery by one of our water trucks. Don't know how long we shall be here as I understand we are waiting the unloading of our transport when it does arrive. My turn for the wash tub. Remember me to all. I'll be with you again soon. N.

It is noticeable that since landing, all out-going correspondence is censored by No 2880 and franked by the Army Post Office.

APO

It's Saturday night, just before supper and a few minutes in which to write you. Yesterday, after a bit of drill and lecture during the morning, we had a half day off. A third of the company went into town or the nearest resemblance to one. I wasn't one of them. The lads had a few queer tales to tell on returning, so I went out this afternoon on a like errand, but after walking about a mile in the sun and waiting on the roadside for two hours for a lift, returned to tea without further exploration. Going out I came across a grand big house and farm adjoining with the usual orange and lemon orchard. In the grounds was a small dairy herd, some long-eared, long-tailed sheep and two mares. Something like a grasshopper jumped on to one of the fruit trees, (it was at least three inches long), and further along a huge black and grey toad six inches across. I am now awaiting a pink elephant!

Our first lot of mail arrived today. Supper time draws near – an innovation started last night and tonight it's Irish stew.

28 March 1943

6.30ish

I go on twelve hour guard at 7.00 p.m. We double up our guard after dark now when on active service. We've had torrential rain until just before tea and after a full night of it too. It is like a quagmire. Lectures and brains trust took up the morning and this afternoon attended a religious service. Whilst waiting for this service to start we watched the natives killing a sheep. The padre read the lesson, 'As sheep to the slaughter'. Funny, eh?

87

I see on orders that the air graph service is to start on 1st April. Ordinary letters can go by air mail for 10d. (4p). If funds allow I may do this. I certainly shall to Mum and Dad probably tomorrow. Time's up to drop pen and grab rifle. All love, N.

It hurt me such a lot when N. didn't seem to get the letters I'd sent – must have been awful for him.

31 March 1943

Arrival of the thirteen-pager

Although I got a 10d. (4p) ordinary letter off by air mail to Mum and Dad, I see on orders that the method is cancelled. Our air graph system starts tomorrow and should get to you quicker, though circumstances may alter the speed. Yesterday we got our NAAFI issue, more or less what we asked for. I received a tablet of soap, bottle of beer, seventy cigs, bar of chocolate and tin of blacking for Fr. 50. or 5s. (25p). So not so bad. This morning I've been up to the office and made you an extra allotment of 1s. 3d. a day – that's 8s. 9d. (43p) per week. So look out for it, dear, and it's dated from 31st March. I'm workshop's medical orderly – our company MO is down with dysentery so I've his job until he returns. Up to press I've only had blistered feet, waxed ears, cut fingers, stings and boils to attend to and practically nothing to work with. In fact all I have is cotton wool, gauze, one six inch bandage, half-inch bandage, bottle aspirins, scissors, a tin of sticking plasters and a tin of health salts. So tomorrow I go in to town to see what I can scrounge from the hospital, the one I visited the other night when I took a case in with a beautiful temperature and headache. He was put in the isolation tent – all tents on the top of the hill have army MOs, orderlies and English trained nurses with the rank of lieutenant and

88

two pips up.

The weather has improved and is definitely warmer. The mud is beginning to dry up so we aren't so bad. Up to yesterday we had been nearly floating in slosh and thick mud. Only the main roads are metalled, all the rest just mud. In the rainy season nearly impassable and in summer hard-baked and very dusty. We have a wireless here. Well, the higher up have so we get the news and also bulletin daily on the notice-board and it looks as if things are moving with us now, doesn't it? Hope so anyway. I'm short of materials for packing up some oranges and lemons for you but will do when I can. Round here dogs are barking all night long and frogs croaking sound as big as buckets – a cross between a ratchet and a goat bleating. The company is still getting an odd air mail which must have been written as soon as we left, a thing I forgot to tell you. Of course you will be longing for my letters as I am for yours. Come Sunday it's a month since saying goodbye at the station – it seems so much longer. I may get chance to write more later.

1 April 1943

Another beautiful morning and getting hotter. Just finished a morning round 'on feet'. Thought I'd have to hitch-hike into town but now I'm to go by transport with the quarter master after dinner.

2 April 1943

The MO came and after seeing his cases we had a brains trust, dinner, then off for supplies. Got into town about 3.00 p.m. and walked up to the hospital. It had got awfully warm. My visit turned out OK and I'm to pick up the supplies I've ordered tomorrow. Had a look at the chap I'd taken into isolation. Seems he has tonsilitis, but waiting for the result of the throat swab. I had a look round town, bought some cards, ink and envelopes for the lads and about 5.00 p.m. ran into Bailey and Curry, so of course we had a drink – what queer stuff, no beer, just wines, all colours. Some tasting like vinegar, some like port at Fr.3 (about $3\frac{1}{2}$d. – 2p). We went for a meal which cost about 2s. (10p). Of course we had to have more wine, in fact a bottle of champagne between us. We began to rock a bit but we eventually got back at a respectable hour. A rotten head and filthy mouth this morning. I do wish you could see some of these places, the people and their ways, the horse-drawn pulleys, bullock carts, careering buses packed to the doors – Arabs sat all over the roof. One I saw had a driver with a blonde French girl sat on his knee, arms round his neck, kissing him. How he managed to drive I don't know, but he did and well over our speed limits. The usual Arab pedlar has been round with his oranges, four for Fr. 10. (3d. each – 1p). Lovely sweet juicy oranges. I'm loath to leave you. All love, N. PS. No post have arrived yet.

3 April 1943

Air Graph

Actually I'm nearly stumped for news. Have just finished an eighteen pager which I've been jotting down in this last three days. Our mail is still arriving in driblets, none for me as yet. I'm not unduly worried. Have you been able to get something done about felling those two beeches on the plot? Let me know what you can and how you are faring. Space is soon filled on these graphs. Keep smiling. N.

4 April 1943

Air Letter

Sunday night and a bit of breathing space. This job isn't very hard, but I'm always on the go. We are getting shipshape here now and I should imagine will move up nearer the fighting area before long. I've managed a most beautiful bath in a bucket since dinner and all clean clothes on and dirty ones washed. One of our lads has had mail taking only five days and this his eighth. I'm longing for some mail from you. I know you will be writing with your usual skill, so speed the day when the mail arrives with letters from you. Always with you, N.

17 April 1943

Note new address: 2160917 Spr Bell N
258 Corp Fld Pk Coy Re
British North African Forces

Received your air mail of the 6th. It took only ten days, the first I've had from you. Excuse poorness of ink, it is difficult to get and have to water it down. Your letter was grand and I was thrilled to bits, it took me about ten minutes before I opened it – I was ecstatic. Johnny Hoare's wife has had a daughter. Eileen staying at Mrs A.'s has a son. Contrary to you our weather is scorching hot. We have moved on into more fertile country. No flies etc., but plenty of ants. We are expecting a further move to our final object, the coast around Tunis, which we aren't a hundred miles from.

18 April 1943

Sunday morning and have moved again. Late last night I'd two letters from home. Four from you and I'll reply in due course. I've only one want at the moment – will you send powder or tablets to make lemon drinks. The water is treated but doesn't taste too good. Limited space, limited time. As always, N.

23 April 1943

Green letter

It's Good Friday morning after a night of heavy rain and even large hail-stones, but the sun is up and it is hot once again. The big push started Wednesday night – during the night. I was out all day with the sick, etc., and visited a CCS (Casualty Clearing Station) and a general hospital, both of which were full of our lads back from this new clash. In fact they were coming in in an endless procession, poor beggars, bandaged up all ways. None complained however. Maybe too beat for words. I felt how paltry my few sick compared with these. Still, all sick need attention.

The Eighth Army is gallantly fighting. The greatest fighting machine in the world today. I'd like to tell you that we, the Ninth Corps, who are in the First Army, assisted them and around Pichon in no small way. There was an order of the day issued from Alexander which is still on the notice board, personally thanking us and now in the fighting in front of Tunis they have come up to help us. It is us who are bearing the main attack. Most of the casualties I saw yesterday were the Hampshires, which are our infantry. All of which means, dear, that although our company aren't doing much actual

92

fighting, we are busy at the thick of it. We are to get the emblem of the 1st Army – a white shield with a red cross and sword. We have a new Corps sign – a herald's trumpet, the idea being from a biblical quotation: Should the trumpet sound, get cracking, I think.

This part is rather a hilly wilderness; even grass won't grow, only weeds and stuff like gorse-thorn trees whose spikes are about three inches long and a few stunted trees. The surface is rocky outcrop and sandy soil. The dry sandy roads send up clouds of filth for miles. Ants by the million, scorpions occasionally; a spider grey in colour that I dug out of a hole alongside my tent was at least three inches overall. There are any amount of tortoises by all the filthy streams. It is poorly populated, only a few Arabs here and there with their dogs, mules, donkeys and hens. To see them on the road the man rides ahead, also the sons, if they have a mount; then they trail off in descending order, women last carrying great loads on heads and backs, besides any too young to walk.

We are able to get most of our needs from the NAAFI but not ink or decent writing paper. Goodbye, happy thoughts. All love, N.

28 April 1943

Air Letter

I've so much mail from you now, and to answer, that I'll never get through it. Your photo arrived at the weekend and looks wistfully at me from the sideboard.

We are bothered an awful lot with fleas, scratch, scratch. Our allowance for writing is limited to about one a week of either an air graph or air letter. I'm always anxious that you hear from me as soon as there's an issue.

Air Graph

It's a week since I last wrote you. I've been waiting in vain for an air letter as I cannot get much on these. Have been here about a week. There was a lot of air activity when we first arrived but this has now diminished and it's quite comfortable, touch wood.

It's over a week since I'd any mail from you and longing for your next long epistle. On your next weekend off, will you remind Jack and Wing that they owe me a letter.

With regards to me, I'm fine. I have an interesting job which makes all the difference, a good billet, even a bed, sideboard, table and chairs. Had an Arab in this morning with a most beautiful septic shrapnel wound in the back, stinking like Hell and oozing pus like a dripping tap. Having dressed it, I have sent him to the hospital for more treatment. Every day there are many minor ailments amongst our company and now also an attachment of RASC and Pioneers, so I've a large family. I almost forgot, but I'm able to have a vase of roses on my table. There is an actual garden here and roses flourish, all colours and smelling so lovely – takes me back to home and you. Until another day. All love, N.

8 May 1943

I'd no sooner got my air graph off to you than your mail arrived. (25 March, 21 and 24 April). Sorry to note you haven't been receiving mine too well. You seem to be having patches of drama and accidents to cope with and you must get very tired climbing that hill every day. We are a working unit, dear, and behind the lines. Bizerta and Tunis fell yesterday and all is going according to plan and before long you will be hearing of the fighting men having turned Jerry and his tribe out of the country altogether. I wonder what then. Our drivers and dispatch riders report the most colossal collection of material left by Jerry everywhere. Guns loaded just as they had been using them with no time for demolitions, so it is a tremendous success. Time is up. Take care, always in my thoughts. N.

14 May 1943

Air Graph

The post has just arrived but none for me. We have moved again. It's a lovely place – a seaside resort, miles of sand and deserted bathing huts. We get a dip each day, it's glorious and warm, but very salty. I've been twice into the city. What a sight, flags all over, flowers, embraces, with all kinds of allied troops and colours and packed out with military vehicles. It's a lovely change to be amongst people and houses, grape vines and trees again after the dirt and sand of the places of late. Of course it won't last. We are bound to be moved somewhere – we are at war, not play. Had your letter of 28 April on Monday last. No space to answer. Will as soon as possible. That's all sweetheart, Bye, N.

19 May 1943

Air Letter

Not unduly worried but still no mail for ten days. Since the air graph I have sent off a rather lengthy epistle by ordinary mail. On Monday we finished works at dinner time and set off to play one of our field companies at football in the afternoon. A matter of thirty odd miles away and managed to get ourselves lost and went seventy six miles round. Apart from missing the match was the possibility of winning and cigarettes as prizes. I didn't mind at all as it was a beautiful afternoon and our route took us winding right along the coast, looking down on the bay with its famous blue waters and palm trees. Yesterday we again finished at dinner time and played an intersectional match on an improvised pitch at our camp. Quite good sport and we won 3-0.

Today we finish again at dinner time and twenty of us are going into town on a victory parade. Don't know what the procedure will be or who will be there. We may even get on the newsreel. I'm writing this sat in the truck at the CCS, having brought our sick, which I do every day, so excuse pencil. The clearance station is now taken over for medical cases – the campaign being over, no more battle cases to come back. It is just outside the village at which we understand Von Armin was captured. There is still a flood of rumours going the rounds. I'll let you know our future movements when possible.

We have the whoppingest POW camp in the adjoining field to us. Germans in one, Italians in a second and civilian internees in a third sections. It's queer to see them all. Yesterday a fighting machine, today like cattle behind a few coils of wire and I think it says a lot for our leaders and troops. We appear to have taken Jerry completely by surprise, but there it is. Good strategy and good boys to carry it out.

Knowing that our mail is censored is somewhat off-putting. My letters do not seem to make much mention of you, but you know you are the central figure in my life. All love, N.

Green letter passed by Censor

Somehow I feel like writing so be prepared. Firstly I sent you an air graph yesterday to keep you posted but you know how little I can get on it, so I'll start by answering your last to me of the 28 April. You say that you now know where we are but I wonder do you, so I'll start at the beginning.

We left Avonmouth up the Bristol Channel on the Sunday dinner time, having gone on board on Friday, your birthday, and steamed up to the Clyde, arriving on the Monday evening. Here we picked up our convoy and left in the early hours of Tuesday. We sailed out of the Clyde into mid-Atlantic and then changed course west of Ireland and right down until off Spain and for the Mediterranean. We passed Gibraltar about 1.00 a.m. so I didn't see it at all. When my first trip on deck came along we were steaming off the coast of Spain with snow-capped mountains overlooking us. Of course we were out well too far to distinguish anything and still carrying out convoy manoeuvres, as had been going on all through the voyage. Sometimes we were roughly in four or five lines abreast and at others any old how in appearance. All the time we were leading vessel on the port bow.

All that day we had the European coast in sight, then we went south. I was on the Bren gun all night and was unfortunate to see one of our ships go west – the only one. Jerry sent out aircraft each day and after the third day we were picked up by subs. What with that and approaching enemy territory we manned all our small arms as well as the ship's guns.

This last night a sub sent a torpedo at us which passed only fifteen feet in front of our bows, behind the next ship and then in front of a third and did no damage. The destroyers were soon dashing about but I didn't think they got the sub. An aircraft dropped a torpedo and it got the next ship to us in the stern. She dropped out of convoy with one destroyer escort and eventually sank at 5.00 p.m. that evening. All troops were taken off, including WAAFs and two of our field companies. One or two had been killed by the explosion, none lost from drowning. We eventually docked on the Tuesday dinner time in Algiers, ten days after leaving. A beautiful day and a beautiful sight from a distance. Disembarked at 2.00 p.m. We marched with full kit and blankets to a farm some twenty miles distance, St Phillip by name, south of Maison Carree. A small mixed French and Arab township. Here we stayed awaiting the arrival of our trucks until a fortnight had passed. We then set off on our long trek up to the fighting.

Our first day took us right up into the beginning of the Atlas mountains, a distance of over a hundred miles. What a sight! Eagles overhead, snow-capped peaks, sheer drops of thousands of feet. All the time we were winding up and up. The second day was much the same, still going up and over. We were unlucky enough to have a big workshop truck burnt out, our distance travelled being a 130 miles in all this day. Third day saw us nearly over the main chain but by now it was bitterly cold each night and a cold wind all day; not quite so far covered this time. Fourth day was bad, we didn't make camp until 11.30 p.m., terribly hungry, dirty and cold. Fifth day was all desert as had been the latter part of the previous day; nothing but filth, cacti and flies. It was a memorable occasion for we arrived at our destination of Pichon about 9.00 p.m. and made camp under some stunted trees. On our first day here we were getting cleared up, tanks moving up, artillery fire, wounded coming back was continuous, corpses, graves, all the aftermath of battle was everywhere. The Hampshires and Sixth Armoured Division had only cleared the place of Axis forces the day before we arrived, our first experience of a major clash. Perhaps you will remember in your papers the mention of Pichon and picture us, the Ninth Corps pushing forward ever forward. We only stayed four days in Pichon as the Eighth Army pushing up from the march line relieved us, so off we went again, this time north. If you care to look up the map, this journey took only two days. The first night I spent taking a dispatch rider into hospital with a broken shoulder after a spill. The second night I was on guard but what a tonic the next day! I received my mail from you and on top of that got my own quarters and full time job. Exempt from all duties except guard. Next day, Saturday 17 April, I got seven letters and all was right with the world.

This place was Sidi Ayed. Nothing really except a station without a platform, but we spent better days and nights here out in the open away from trees and flies, which had bothered us considerably at Pichon. Stings and bites were so numerous I ran out of disinfectants to deal with them all. I'd collected a beauty of a sting on my eye so was soon out scouring for more medical supplies, which I'm always doing now.

After ten days at Sidi Ayed the Axis was retreating so quickly we were off again, this time only a one day trip to another farm between Bon-Arada and Goublat. We were nearly on top of Jerry and had bombing raids every day and night in fact, too near to be pleasant. Still he was going back. We stayed here from 25 April till 11 May. Last Tuesday we left with few regrets. Tunis had fallen, so had Bizerta. We came south to this place, St Germain, where we are now basking in the sunshine, bathing in the Mediterranean, doing very little work.

Prisoners are everywhere and all sorts of materials, I've boxes of 'his' medical stuff and we are using umpteen trucks and cars of his too. That brings us up to date, I think. Of course you know Von Arnim is a prisoner. All is finished in this theatre. We wonder what will happen next to us. We are under canvas and your photo is in my pocket. Whilst at Goublat, I'd a room in the farm to myself and your photo in a place of honour. I'm glad you've managed to see *In Which We Serve*. What is this about drivers and bus conductors going on strike? Send the buggers out here! I wonder if they've ever thought what would happen should we, the Navy and Air Force refuse duty for another penny an hour or half longer in bed or a shorter week and holidays with pay.

Bailey is one of the three wireless operators and, like me, at HQ. Curry is in field stores and still back at our last place loading materials for the dump. He had all his kit, personal and army, all his money and photos of his wife destroyed when one of our trucks was shot up by Jerry and set on fire. Curry wasn't with it, but he had been sleeping in it with three more of their section. That day the truck was out with two drivers picking up spares and replacements off wrecks, when they nearly ran into Jerry's lines. They were hit in the back and engine and made a bolt for it. One returned the same day with the story, but the other was taken prisoner and sent back to Tunis by the Africa Corps, Herman Goering's crack troops, but when we got into Tunis, he was released and was sitting on the roadside wondering what to do, when one of our trucks passed. So they picked him up and brought him back fit and well and terribly hungry, a week's growth on his chin, Jerry tunic on his back and an Italian rifle over his shoulder. I shall always think him lucky. He's a great lad from Manchester, all smiles, and he's courting a Sunderland girl.

Time for bathing. I'll finish when I get back. Had a good tea after a marvellous splash. You would glory in it. The water is lovely and warm and clear. Don't know the future, but I'll let you know all I can as soon as possible. All love, N.

25 May 1943

Air Mail

Another week seems to have passed without me getting you written. Your letters of the 3rd, 8th and 13th have arrived, which bring great joy. I think I'd told you of our impending victory march through the town. We left camp in the afternoon for the other side of town. Had tea and supper and then bedded down, for the night. We were up early next morning, all clean and sparkling, and moved off eventually around dinner time. We marched in right through town, passed the saluting base with all the nobs and in the following order I believe, though I didn't see much myself – I was too busy trying to look good: French, American and British, a party from all units concerned in the fighting. We got back in time for tea and a little tired.

Work is easier now and most afternoons have a splash in the Med. We have played a good deal of football in the evenings – last night the Rifle Brigade, whom we beat 2-0. It is now seven weeks since I made your extra allotment. If it hasn't come through, write to the paymaster about it. It's high time it had.

Many times in quiet moments I plan. The latest is the drive to our plot. Your little prayer for me made me cry. It was what I needed and so like you. God bless. Keep safe for me. All love, N.

4 June 1943

Green Letter

My anniversary today. One whole year in the army. Seems a life time and yet we have men who have been in fourteen years and lads who joined the territorials just prior to the war at eighteen and who have been in nearly four years, never known what it was to draw a man's wage and are veterans at twenty two or three. So I can't grumble can I?

This is an ordinary mail as I haven't an airmail. Next will be an air graph. It gets to you so much quicker. I've managed ordinary letters off to my regulars and thanked Mrs H's committee for a 7s. 6d. (37½p) postal order.

No letter from you since the 29th May. I'm longing for your next. In my last letter I said we have moved. We're busy constructing and have dozens of Italian prisoners labouring for us – it doesn't affect me. We have a big general hospital in town and two more in the erection stage not far from us. All carry QAVNR, (Queen Alexander's Voluntary Nursing Reserve) sisters. I've heard they are good lasses.

In poor Betty's air graph to me it would cause you some amusement, I'm sure. I know I shouldn't remark about her but, bless her, it was so funny. Her address took up just under half the available writing space. She started with the old phrase, 'I hope this finds you as it leaves me at present.' Her spelling wasn't too good. About all she said was, 'I went to a wedding and came back' – rather obvious, and 'Cynthia has been up and took everything out of my basket' which, to say the least, interested me immensely. I tried to be interesting in my reply. You can, if you wish, pull her leg about us both corresponding.

Bill D. said he thought he would have a service number by the time I had his letter. You would have split your sides with laughing if you had read my reply, but it was how we used to talk to each other.

Camels are an everyday sight now and yesterday I saw a white one. Grass snakes are shedding their skin, which doesn't stretch as they grow, so a new skin is underneath as they cast it. Ants by the million working all hours of the day. Spiders with a leg span of about three inches. Very few birds. Glow worms which have wings and fly out at night are then stationary on long grass with the last three cells in their bodies glowing with a green phosphorus light, which I have observed at least thirty yards away.

We are back out of town on a more or less flat, rocky, scrub-covered plain. A few olive trees are planted and plenty of prickly cacti, a little corn sown by the natives, a few blades of grass, a great deal of sun and a good deal of dust. We were much relieved when orders were published stating we were to have two half days a week where possible, Wednesday and Sunday. One for swimming, the other for rest, washing and sewing etc., and starting this week. I missed the swimming, having to take a burn case into dock. Here we can get a few eggs, big melons and small peaches. They taste very good and we have a mess tin on, stewing some for this evening. Our rations are still quite good, generally a little bacon for breakfast with porridge and slice of bread, sometimes Spam or tinned sausage. Dinner a light meal at 12.00 p.m. Sometimes bread and cheese and treacle. Today tomatoes and sliced onions – raw. Tea at 7.00 p.m. is the big meal. Beef fritters or pie, stew or meat and veg pie. Puddings such as jam roll, rice pud, plum pie, so it's really very good. Do you remember the stew you used to make in a big brown pot? Many moons ago. All love, N.

5 June 1943

Air Graph

Haven't had an air mail issue lately and nothing from you for over twelve days. I am sending this as a makeshift after a long letter to you yesterday and to give you the name and address of a corporal's girl who will exchange news should there be lapses of anxious times on either side. Etta Rainford, etc. I'm feeling fine now after a touch of dysentery over a period of a week. Although I didn't feel too good and it was uncomfortable, I managed to keep going. We are still in the same place, still busy though I cannot tell you what at. That you are well and happy is my continual wish. Have no worries about me. Take care. Love me always, N.

Air Mail

A week tomorrow since I wrote you and I'd no sooner handed it in than I received your first air graph to me, dated 21 May. An air graph from Jack A. Had a short open air service and finished the day with a quiz. Have managed some football, the ground just hard stones similar to an English road after being tarred and dressed with granite chips. It's all they can do out here. The ground was properly marked out, had a stand and was walled in – a stadium so called.

Had a graph and mail from you and glad you had managed a trip over to Mum's. So our photos are prominently displayed. I'll only whisper this, it's a habit my Mum has of placing visitors' photos on view the day before a visit. I'm busy in spurts and find I am writing a very dull letter. All love, N.

15 June 1943

Air Graph

Your letter of the 5th arrived and I'd just begun this to you when the truck picked us up to go into town to the Garrison Theatre. I don't think it was entirely suited to its audience but it got us a break for three hours. Keep up the letters to me. Love, N.

Air Mail

Yet another week has lapsed since I wrote you last. I'd been waiting this issue and didn't hear from you until yesterday. So far this month I've had your letters of the 3rd, 7th and 11th. Let me know what your trip to the Blue John Mine was like and get it right about the difference of the stalagmite and stalactites in the formation, as I can never remember. Believe I've already asked you for fountain pen nibs. Plus that, will you send me a tin of Andrews, a jar of our special shaving cream and a tube of MacLeans? I didn't expect that you would fancy the Chester trip, though I assure you, you would have a good time. It really is a lovely old place and North Wales too. I wish you would consider it, as you are unlikely to get a holiday break with me for some time. Even though we both long to get lost somewhere together to forget everybody and everything. No, I didn't see Churchill or the King on his visit here, nor did I manage to see Leslie Howard's *First of the Few*, but I believe it's a smashing picture. I've sent off another parcel of lemons to you. Green ones this time, hoping they will ripen on the way. Yours, N.

B Johnson Censor on most letters. Then there's some one called A Hague – or really looks like A Haggis!

26 June 1943

Air Mail

Saturday afternoon and just another day. Remember how at this time I'd be with you on the train for an odd glorious weekend together. Did it matter about the rain, snow or even worse, not it, we were together, that's what really mattered.

Caught a scorpion of the yellow variety the other day and a spider of the poisonous group, both of which my good friend the MO disposed of by anaesthetic. My job has swelled somewhat in size, if not importance. I'm still one of the lowest paid in the company. I have to see that all the various sectional cookhouses, latrines, urinals, ablutions and areas are clean and hygienic. See that every man gets his ascorbic acid pill each evening, his atabrine or mepacrine on Monday, Tuesday, Thursday and Friday evenings. To get rid of all breeding places of flies and mosquitos. Control of any waste and stagnant water. To know all there is to know about the above subjects, I've been wading through literature and dreaming of hygiene, malaria, anopheles, larvae, pupae, carriers, chains, paris green, fumigation and the Lord knows what and then, of course, I have the common or garden everyday sick, lame and lazy to attend to. Also another job which has come my way is the NAAFI. Two of us run it. We buy in bulk each Wednesday from the nearest base sufficient rations for the whole company. On bringing back, price it, sell it to the sections as required, probably the next day. When we have them all satisfied, which takes a bit of doing, we cash up, check, balance, get an officer's signature and are then ready for next week. It means a hell of a good temper with the lads. It was bedtime when we had finished and the turn over in the region of Fr. 12896. I'm afraid that as usual I've contrived to write about myself and space filled. Love as always, N.

29 June 1943

Air Graph

Tuesday evening and the sun is setting after a very hot day. They seem to be getting hotter, but we have a little breeze from the sea. An air graph from Etta R says she hasn't heard from you yet. No change here. Kept rather busy one way or another. Love, N.

Air Mail

Have received your twelve pager of 21 June, air mail of 20 June and ten pager of 11 June in that order. I've been wondering for ages if you had received my allotment but could never remember to ask. All the others who made them have had notification. So glad it's through. How did they come to send you my income tax papers? Hope your cousin Jack will soon be released from his prison camp. I wish him well when next you write him. Keep writing me, although I've not a lot of time to answer all you have written about. So forgive. What with patrols and guards and normal duties there hasn't been, chance to concentrate and do you the justice you deserve. Love always, N.

7 July 1943

Air Graph

Haven't been able to get started with a long letter yet. Have had several mails and 200 Player's cigarettes from a Sheffield firm. Do you know how this has come about? Are you responsible? It was a complete surprise and I'm grateful for same.

Yesterday was a 'B', our first taste of what the natives call a sirocco – a terrific wind and clouds of sand continually from the early hours until dusk. Tents down, temperatures up, everybody absolutely wet through with perspiration. This storm coming from hundreds of miles of scorching hot desert. Dry hot burning heat – almost unbearable. Everything covered in filth, even the drinking water was hot. We are back to normal today, though still hot yet a wee breeze from the sea and I'm hoping for a swim this afternoon. All love, N.

Green Letter

A lovely cool morning. It's 5.00 a.m. and just beginning to get light. Freshness and the scent of your letter is all around me. Your confirmation that my letters to you are interesting is a tonic.

Forget about arguments going on about wedding presents simply because my relatives weren't invited to our wedding. I don't give a damn. Under the circumstances you would think they would understand – it's so stupid. Mother, I should think, expected we could have done more. Aunt Emma is sincere and as you know, wants to send something.

We've been playing football again and still got gravel rash on my knees from the so-called field. I know very little of the medical terms. You call it dispensing, I call it knocking something up. Flavin is one tablet to 2oz of fluid. Iodine one capsule to equal parts methylated spirit and Water Glauber. Salts one in three as an aperient or as a lotion for cleaning up wounds as a dressing. Sodi Mag the same (Epsom salts). We have Sodi Bic, Kaolin, Calamine, Pot Permang and then I get lost amongst the MISTS: Mist Aspirin, (gargle), Mist Tussis Nig, (cough), Mist Expect, Mist Ferri Arsen and Mist Ferri Stric, both tonics. Chlor et Morph for tummies. There's Codeine tabs, Dovers tabs, Menthol nasal drops, Menthol crystals for inhalation. Two sorts of ear-drops. Lead and opium and Mist APC – that I almost forgot. No, I haven't a medical book of any description, but would you send me, as you suggested, because it is so compact, a Brailles Nursing Diary. It must be small. Something in medicine and bandaging if possible, but none of your books. You must not send any. I have very little room for storage when we move. However I do thank you for your thoughtful kindness.

For God's sake, I hope you will not be using dishcloth stuff for vests when I come home.

How I wish I'd married you sooner, as I'd always intended, with the woman I loved! But you had a career and I was quite selfish in mine. Instead I now have a guilty conscience and a longing for what might have been.

Since my previous part of the letter. I've obtained a book from one of the orderlies at the hospital RAMC, (Royal Army Medical Corps). Training on anatomy, physiology and first aid – the latter a great help.

Our reveille is at 4.30 a.m. and first parade 05.00 a.m., breakfast 7.30 to 8.00 a.m., morning break 10.00 to 10.15 a.m., lunch 13.00 p.m., tea 17.30 p.m. We are finished by this time and can go swimming, but today is my 'off day' and have tried to sleep it off without success. Last night we had a military band concert for our benefit, choosing not to go but heard it in the distance. Instead I was making up Flavine and getting a good wash down after which I felt a whole lot better. Had to take the NAAFI down to our field stores section about five miles away and saw Bill Curry, bless him.

The company is going in small parties to a rest camp for three days. Already two lots have returned. The CSM says we are going in order of the amount of work done. So naturally I'll be the last batch, he says. I wouldn't be surprised – in fact it will suit me better, so long as I do get before we move on. Here it's a small bay of a little coastal town and there are several shops. Water melons and lemonade can be bought. You should taste the melons – I've eaten dozens lately.

I have to take the sick by 7.00 a.m. each morning and need to clean out my medicine chest. It's a constant job keeping the filth down and trying to keep clean. I love you, N.

Just sent an air graph to Mum and Dad. I owe them a letter but I'm damned if I can settle down to it. Two more of your letters to hand. Thanks for the parcel you are sending and I'm wondering what else. Don't spend your hard-earned cash on me. Glad you have put the tree felling into Jackson's hands. He can do what we cannot. Send me the site measurements and building line so that I can work on them.

You will know of our invasion of Sicily and probably more than we do. Though we helped to make it possible we get little news. Although I do believe everything is going to plan, which says a hell of a lot. We now spend most afternoons in the Med after 1.30 p.m. What a job though, getting up at 4.00 a.m. We have had a good report from our inspection on Sunday and seven of us went to a smashing ENSA show. When we came here we were told it was for about six weeks and that is up tomorrow. Our jobs are through and work slack. We all expect moving soon, just where we don't know. There is a build-up for an invasion and would seem a matter of days before it comes off. We have been preparing for this in every way. We definitely won't be in the first or second wave as we haven't been able to do anything for ourselves, either trucks, gear or men. Our support must have had some real value. Have I mentioned seeing *Will Fyfe*? He was very good and blew our trumpets for us. Away now, Love, N.

23 July 1943

Air Graph

Over a week since I last wrote you but I've a good excuse this time. Have had three days at the 'holiday camp'. Now this sounds very grand; in fact it is in a way, but oh dear, how like the army – the officers can go to Tunis, which is now in full swing shops, theatres, pictures, hotels, street-cars, canteens with beer and wines on ice – but we have had to go on a cliff top three miles away doing exactly nothing. No habitation or entertainment of any description, just the sea. Now I grant you, three days' rest is more than I expected and very lucky to get this, but it could have been so much better. Decent food and messing. What we most lacked was beer or at least lemonade. Hope I haven't bored you with my belly-aching. We have spent most of the time in the sea or rambling on the rocks. On our last evening we went for a swim as the moon came up and arrived back here at 10.00 a.m. You know the mess after leaving someone in charge. They must have had a war on three inch bandages – I'd left thirty two. A Winchester of Flavine stock down to nil. No letter from you since the 14th, that's nine days ago. A letter from Mum and Dad tells me of your visit. I've tried to sleep and perspiration rolls off even as I write. All love, N.

25 July 1943

Green Letter

Must try and write a decent long letter. The temperature at midday was 165° in the sun, in shade 126° and late evening 104°. So you may be able to appreciate our discomfort. We had an impromptu concert last week, grand little dos. Everybody is called upon to give a little turn, whilst vino flows fairly freely. Quite a lot of community singing, a good few filthy jokes and a lot of turns from the lads. Some good, some moderate and some definitely terrible, but all got a good hand. As you will have guessed, I'm working up to telling you that I've tried to do my bit and was moderately successful. I did quite a bit before I met you, but somehow being over-awed by you, my talents disappeared. I must admit it brought out others, dear, so I've rendered in my tenor voice some of the songs I danced to, such as 'Charmain,' 'The Desert Song,' 'One Alone,' 'Passion Flower,' 'Sweethearts,' 'Maid of the Mountains,' 'I'll See You Again,' etc. If you can get me some song books, I'd be pleased – musical comedy hits.

The following day being Sunday, we had a little service amongst ourselves. One chap read the lesson, another a most beautiful prayer, a third a brief sermon, with about half a dozen hymns. It rather made us feel good.

Of course I've already told you about the rest camp, if it hasn't already been censored out, but I feel very angry. It was most beautiful there in the clear water of the sea. The bottom was always visible, all crazy patterns on the pebbles and sand caused by the sun's reflection. Small fish swam in shoals – blowed if I could catch one. The natives were catching squid and small octopi, which sent out an inky cloud on disturbance. An electric eel stung one of our chaps. Camels and mules were drinking and being washed and the native women doing their washing by dipping, then rubbing in clay from the cliffs, stamping and beating most thoroughly and finally rinsing well. You should just see the result – perfectly white.

One morning when swimming before breakfast we went round a corner and came upon about a dozen women doing their ablutions and washing small children, all in the nude, and wasn't there a scuffle. We retired gracefully so as not to embarrass them too much. We swam most of the day and by moonlight it was marvellous. Wish you had been with me. I have collected a few shells as a memento of Tunisia and the blue Med. Water melons are at their peak just now, quite luscious. The juice gets all over the face and into ears as we scoff them. Lemons are finished. A poor class of apple is in. Pears and plums are in, also almonds. Had an air graph from Cousin Jack who said you looked fit and well. Haven't heard from you for eleven days. They must be held up somewhere, as I know you'll be writing. Heard from Wing and that Stan and Hoppy are on holiday in Edinburgh. Our weather has broken; heaps of lightning which fired overhead some barrage balloons. Rain in the evening brought cooler air.

I must have a letter from you before I go any further. We do so look forward to mail from home. The joy on a chap's face when he does and the utter disappointment when he doesn't. Bye, Dear.

Thursday after tea

I believe I said this letter would stray over a day or two. I have been excused from duties, being off colour with coryza. Coughing and spitting filth, my head felt like a solid block and I've never had such headaches or felt so ill for a long time. Backache, high temperature, sweating and unable to sleep. My head jumped off my shoulders when I stood up. I'm fit again and only told you because it is a relief to do so. Many of the lads have been ill in varying degrees.

After moaning about getting no mail from you, the fifteenth and eighteenth letters arrived. Sorry the lemons arrived bad, because you said they are not available in the shops at home. Think you would like Etta Rainford. She writes me little notes and is full of fun. You will find something in common as she is a keen tennis player too. You will understand after seeing *Desert Victory* what has happened and, like me, you will wonder how life can go on after seeing the terrific bombardment – attack after attack and there are still men running forward as if in perpetual motion. How humans can stand the strain is a remarkable thing to me and it says a lot for the normal human make-up.

We have a lad here from Burnley who has a small farm. He saved me a seat on the train when returning from leave and was the greatest hearted lad I've ever met. The farm was his own when the army claimed him. His old dad and mother tried to run things, but with inexperience and everybody trying to twist them, he's about broke and has applied for compassionate leave to go home and sell up. If only they had let him stay on his farm, as he would never have made a soldier. As always, N.

113

Air Mail

The incoming postal service is somewhat haywire. It is Sunday evening and August the month I love. We have been here in this place nine weeks and for how much longer we don't know. At midday it is twenty one weeks since I said goodbye to you. Both feeling as flat as a pancake, pretending it was only for a short time. This awful country, its water, filth and flies which are a persistent nuisance. Never have I lost my temper so much and oh to have a change of clothes and to ramble in the countryside we love. To feel well, fresh and bursting with energy. What a tantalizing thought.

Mother cannot understand why you couldn't go to Chester – I can – she said you had half promised and then changed your mind. Dad said you were busy making bilberry jam whilst there on your visit. The promised parcel has not yet arrived. Loving you, N.

5 August 1943

Air Graph

Have had mail from you of 9 and 22 July since writing you last. Half the company were inoculated yesterday and the rest get the needle tonight, then forty eight hours rest. I'm to be done when the company are all well. We've lost again at football, playing against an ackack unit. I meant to get an ordinary mail off to you as I've a few personal things I want to say and so will have more room to expound. Meanwhile, as always, my love to you, N.

Green Letter

Another attempt at a long letter to you. No doubt I'll get interruptions. Firstly, I ought to explain the method of censorship – not being sure if you know how it works. The green letter which we get weekly is the one I like to write to you on a more personal basis. We have to sign on the outside to say that there is nothing incriminating to the war effort in the letter. These are checked at a rate of 1 in 500 at random by officers. The air mail has room for writing on its three pages and like the air graph, each one is censored. The air graph is one single page and photographed to the size of a postage stamp and blown up again on its arrival in England. I strongly object to anyone knowing my private feelings or private matters that I want to discuss with you.

I've been on the carpet twice lately for speaking in strong terms to my mother over a purely personal matter and secondly for complaining to you about our so called 'rest camp'. More interest than is necessary is taken in our mail censorship. What they are supposed to be looking for are facts of place names, figures and information helpful to the enemy.

Your last letter has only taken four days and it is Bank Holiday today. There is your air graph of the 23rd July, having taken sixteen days. Have written and thanked the donors of the cigarettes from Sheffield, as you have said it was not of your doing. It is quite a mystery. I was on guard Saturday night and more inoculations. Friday night was my night for typhus. We had another service amongst ourselves. I read the lesson – Acts 9 v 1-9 if you care to look it up. All my love, N.

Air Graph

Five and a half months since we left our English shore and a load has happened since then. It has mainly been a very packed time, yet dare I say it, it seems to have gone quickly. Your parcel of health salts, more pen nibs, shaving cream and toothpaste have arrived, for which many thanks. Several *John Bulls* and *Sunday Pictorials* from home. Have had two doses of Typhus and the MO took blood from a vein. I believe we are to have our last batch of TAB and TT done. I've managed to swim but it's hard work in this heavily salted water. Doing guard now more often in twos. The locals pinch anything they can carry. Yesterday a lad's trumpet worth £38 went missing. That's all again. Always with you. N.

Air Graph

Had your air graph of the 5th. This took sixteen days and the only word I've had from you in two weeks. I heard there had been a fire at the army post office, so perhaps that's where some have been lost. We recently played the Navy and won 3-1. I now have another job as NAAFI under-manager, CQM's clerk and the medical orderly and there's plenty to do. Managed a swim yesterday afternoon and was working until close on 8.00 p.m. There's a surprise parcel on the way to you. At the moment a dust storm is raging and I'm getting smothered and this after a haircut and wash! Hurry the mail. N.

Air Graph 29 August 1943 and Air Mail 3 September 1943

Ages seem to have passed since I last wrote you and still longer since I heard from you. My reason is that we have moved on into Sicily and we are now 'Central Med. Forces' instead of BNAF, so please use in future letters. Firstly, although we're now in Sicily, I'm not allowed to tell you just when and where we came from. We have only what we stand in, plus arms, greatcoat and one blanket, the trucks not having caught up with us yet, as we came across in a small craft. I have no personal belongings, which of course includes writing material. The graph and mail issued to us on the days of writing and the pen I'd borrowed and thought better of it and the pencil a bit of a mess. In the graphs I've asked you and my people to notify each other when you have heard from me. It's over a week since I wrote you and two weeks since writing home. Will tell you all I can when I can. We are near a lovely bay by a stately mountain. It is a better place than Africa, though somewhat similar. British military money only in use, Italian the native tongue. I wonder how soon it will be 'Central European forces'. Needless to say, dear, I'm longing to hear from you, but doubt if there's a letter until a reply to this. We have moved since we landed and might possibly move again before your mail arrives. Then no doubt there will be another few days hold up.

I'm quite busy all the time with the list of jobs previously mentioned and being busy makes the time fly. So roll on the day and still dream our dreams – this can't last forever. Goodbye, my love, always smiling, N.

Air Graph

Sunday morning and just a little time in which to write. Actually nothing fresh to write. This issue we got last night. We're busy again and settling in. A valley runs across us, planted with orange and lemon trees, grapes, almonds and walnuts and a glorious stream gurgles along. Still haven't got our personal gear and at the moment I'm scoffing peaches or are they apricots. Anyhow they are ten for 1s. (5p). I'm sending a franc note as a souvenir. I was talking to some RAMC chaps here. They said it was fourteen weeks before they had any mail here. Think I'll die if it takes so long. Bailey is here, but we have had to leave Curry in dock with malaria. I'm very sorry and a little upset as we have been together during all our army career. So I'll have to write to his wife as I'm confident he'll never get back to us. Everything in the war world or most seems to be going in our favour, the Russians, Pacific and our lads in Italy. It's queer receiving the change from the Sicilians, I believe the lira is valid and stands at about twenty to the shilling. Chin up and take care. N.

8 September 1943

Air Graph

Just sent my second air mail letter to Mum and Dad as I'd felt they may be feeling out of it. I've a few moments to scribble this but a poor substitute as I've so much to tell you. So much to describe. I want so badly to hear from you and know that we are to each other what we always have been. Not that I'm in doubt, but it's nice to hear it. Must be getting morbid. I've spent nights with you and planning 'hideaway' and made ground floor plans and frontage. I even get out and scrape the plans in this soil. Soon it will be time to put the beech

118

seedlings out in the borders. I'm so glad the huge beeches are now down which will help on the ideas we have. That's all, dear, may we soon hear from each other. All my love to you, N.

10 September 1943

Green Letter

I want to talk to you so badly from my heart, but I can't because of the censor, as I've explained before. So I'm not going to try, but add a little note on these cards. I had reckoned on sending them purely of interest value of Sicily. Then I came across these others and thought I was back home and not on a Cooks tour. You will see there is a similarity which reminds me of you and home and walks, etc. Italy is finished and I believe is doing all in her power, if she has any left, to assist us against the Germans. The British and Canadians will be pushing on; the Americans too are in. In the East we are beginning to get somewhere. We still have armies to call on, air mastery is ours and we are supreme upon the sea. Our Russian allies are colossal, no other word describes them, and doubt very much if any of us appreciate the magnitude of the task they faced and are now doing so well. About our local news, no one knows what's in store for us. We're still incomplete, no transport, no nothing. It seems obvious that our next move is Italy, or failing that come home to you, but who knows, we may see the eternal city. It's twelve days since I last wrote from here and the fifth since coming into this country. Will let you know if we look like settling anywhere so that you can send me any little thing I require? The long absence of the trucks may mean they have been pilfered and all my personal belongings being lost, they were all so handy and essential to a fellow's comfort.

We have not heard any more about Curry. Bailey is still with me and waiting to hear from his wife too. We still have a good deal of dysentery and malaria around. We only feel half-baked when normal gear is missing. Even cooking is a problem, with cooks being short of utensils, but we are getting some good food, fruit and veg. I have had one half day since being here. No entertainment of any kind and not allowed out of camp. Anyhow, we haven't any money, but no doubt will be rectified as soon as possible. It's the worst situation we have had to put up with. I've told you all I can. Do hope the African mail catches up soon; it's a fortnight since I heard from you. So I'm longing for the day. All my love, N.

14 September 1943

Air Mail

It's a week and a few hours since I last wrote you, and then only a graph, but I've been so busy that I'm taking this opportunity to get a few lines off. I'm on guard and this is one of my spells of patrol. Fortunately tonight it's a full moon and wondering if it is silvery, bright, beautiful and radiant with you, and isn't it our English harvest moon? I've never told you before, in fact I've told you very little about this island, but we have acres of jasmine growing on our eastern side at an old, or should I say, better type of farm. The smell tonight is most terrifically beautiful. As I walked beside it I was quite intoxicated by its sweetness. Going round the compass on the south side, we have the almond trees in a series of most perfectly straight lines. Whichever way you look the rows are in perfect line. Next door, still south, we have a field of chilli growing plants about potato height. Great, brilliant, red and hanging. Of course I had to taste one and they are the hottest thing I've tasted! With gabbling on about my wonderful surroundings, which incidentally are quite conflicting really, for we have the same damned tribe of flies and heat combined with our main enemies of dysentery and malaria, but on the whole better than Africa. I received your letter of 9 August sent on from BNAF. With little space left, will answer if possible in a green envelope issue and I have so many personal things to say. So bear with me until it arrives in probably a fortnight or so. I am perfectly well and believe you are, so do not worry. All love, N.

17 September 1943

Green Letter

I seem to have so little time to myself now and may not get a decent letter off to you, as intended. I'd no sooner tried to start this than a chappie came in with a boil and very sore toes and the sweatiest feet. Septic sores are quite a job to clean up. I'm clear of them, but it's the lads who suffer so. My time is limited because of my new job. Until just before we left Sousa, the work I'd been given for the last six months, amongst others was medical orderly. It entailed many really dreadful rides in the middle of the night, taking in cases of lousy jobs and losing much sleep. I'm still clerk to the CQ Master and now storeman as well as the medical orderly. Bailey was the other storeman, now he's out. When the ration corporal is out I relieve. Here the night's dressings are arriving. Maurice Matthews, previously mentioned, is good at figures and is the ration corporal, along with Stan Hoole, the company cobbler. We share a bell-tent of our own and sleep on stretchers and in general are very comfortable. The CQMS are only concerned with stores, i.e., food and every article of equipment, clothing, tools, machines and all necessities and storage used by the company. An enormous amount of booking and checking and the like to do. At present we're stock-taking and sorting after the mess left by the previous storeman. This work is 9-5 each day. I do dressings 8-9 each morning and 6.30 p.m. each evening until I get through. So you see that's why I've written you during the night. I've taken into hospital fifteen cases of malaria since in Sicily, also septic cases. I've dozens of others down with septic sores and what a job it is trying to clean them up.

It is now Saturday morning after breakfast and getting a few minutes before dressings start. I've told you about me and now going to grumble. Yesterday three corporals were made up and five lance corporals. The CQMS has only room for one NCO, so I've finished. A railway porter was made up to sergeant and is now a first class fitter. A labourer in a dye works – Lord knows what he is. One a packer at Lewis's, is now the quarter master and so it goes. Yesterday was the best one yet that I've heard – a labourer two years ago built tiled fireplaces and is now made up to third class joiner, why I don't know. Until yesterday he hadn't ever used joiner's tools and can't still. There it is. He was given a piece of wood about nine inches square yesterday and told to plane it up all round and take the corners off and a chamfer all round. This he did to the best of his ability – as expected it was very poor. In fact one of our apprentice kids would have had his behind kicked if he had done it. And what do you think? He's now a second class joiner. That's all the moaning for now, dear, and I'm feeling a bit better for it.

British military money is specially printed when we occupy enemy territory and a limited amount of our ordinary treasury Italian lira and Maltese British currency, both civil and military is used by all. I'm enclosing the promised franc note and some of the colours we were decorated with on entering Tunis, which seems ages ago.

It's Sunday night and quite dark. I'm resolved to write to no-one else but you and home, so it's as well there are no letters from others. They're possibly held up. My temper is still bad. Love you forever, N.

Air Mail 19 September 1943

Sunday Actually I'm in the midst of a long letter to you and have been for three days and what a struggle, being often interrupted or being wanted and it will be like that until dark. So you must forgive if it takes a week or so. Mail is still a mystery, in fact nearly a myth. Your graph of 30 August has arrived in which you tell me of your efforts at mushroom growing. Be sure to have plenty for my return. Your graph is one sent on from Africa so don't know what's happening to the rest. You wouldn't have any idea of the move we had made. Just another indication of our climate – we have managed to obtain a candle and candlestick and mould the wax upright and light it and slowly it collapses into the shape of a walking stick handle. That's how warm it is and it's supposedly the cool of the evening. It really is funny to watch.

Another batch of NCOs were made up yesterday. We, the company, are in good working order and everything going to 'cocker', all the trucks and workshops. No signs of further movement, the lads are pushing on fine in Italy. No further mail from anyone for me. Have managed a half day today and been getting some washing done and getting it clean in cold water. Here's hoping our mail catches up with each other. All love, N.

29 September 1943

It's eight days since I last wrote you and we have moved again. Another sea journey and your guess could be right. I'm still overwhelmed with the reception here at the port and on our journeying we were mobbed and cheered to the echo. It was terrific. All through the country the populace came out to greet us. We were showered with flowers and fruit and could hardly make way. I've managed a photo which I'll send on when chance. Although I'm writing to Mum and Dad, you should get this sooner, so please let them know and that I'm OK. I wasn't worrying about my Dad, dear, and didn't know he had been so ill. Keep a close watch for me. With love always, N.

Green Letter   **Italy**   2 October 1943

It's colossal – there's so much mail from you! There are two which are nearly two months old. No wonder I found it odd when you hadn't replied in conjunction with the line of thought and happenings I'd mentioned. Betty sent an air graph. It was so good I think she must have had some help! A letter from Aunt Emma had taken fifteen weeks. I don't want to refer to 'Miss Fields'. My admiration is for the shows of ENSA, which always gets a crowded audience, be it in the open, luxury theatre or bombed building. They work like hell to give us a little pleasure, suffering hardship almost as the front line men.

Jerry is beaten as sure as God made little green apples and we are cracking him in fine sticks. I've concocted a 'brazier' from a petrol tin – a little smasher, all out of one tin with stand and even three bars to make us feel at home. The fire is going nicely and very handy and can now get some water for washing and warm our feet before turning in and of course it has a mental effect. That reminds me, I haven't had a bath since seeing you last, yet I'm clean. It's surprising what one can do with two pints of water – clean teeth, shave and wash in this order: hands, arms, face and neck, upper body, lower body, legs and feet and finish by rubbing out a pair of socks. As always, N.

Air Graph   5 October 1943

We have been busy moving again. Not far, but it means loading and unloading, so for two days have been in a pickle. No real

124

news to report and we haven't been allowed out yet and I can't get any mail out, as the Army Post Office isn't as far up yet, nor have we received any mail since 23 September and that had been diverted from Africa. So again I'm hoping for a proper bag full. It is much colder at night now and we had a heavy deluge of rain. The sections are billeted in large villas. I am in a double type canvas tent. The main advantage is the privacy it assures me. I have Stan Hoole for a mate, his workshop at one end and my medical things at the other. We are very comfortable. All love, N.

Parcel with letter   9 October 1943

This is your Christmas present. Not very expensive, but I do hope you will like it. The miniature climbing boot is in remembrance of me and I have the other one. When they stand together I'll be with you again. Happy dreams. I'm being a clever lad in getting this off so early and there's a little something for 28 December. My love to you, dearest. N.

Green Letter   Second separate letter on 9 October 1943

I've received your letters of 12 August and 26 September. We're experiencing a rather mixed up post, lacking continuity. Your letter of the 26th was very sweet and full of lovely thoughts, wishes and news. Whilst you were reading *Dragon Seed*, I was reading *House in Exile* by Nora Walm.

Enclosed is a photo of me down in *The Heel*! I'm told they have had terrific storms and winds, uprooting trees. We have escaped so far. We have been in town. The shops are beautifully displayed. Didn't think much to the food we tried. We saw Cary Grant and Katherine Hepburn in the film *Susan*. It was

125

very amusing, but spoken in Italian – it gave me a headache listening to the jabbering. We hitch-hiked back in time for dinner at 5.30 p.m. I'm tumbling into bed after being up all night. I've got clean sheets to sleep in, having had them washed by one of the locals. I'm about to eat a pomegranate and then turn in as tomorrow draws near. All love, N.

Air Mail (Undated)

Had your letter of 20 September 1943. We have been on the move again and hadn't had chance to acknowledge you until now. I can understand your muddled thoughts and the news and cock-eyed letter dates. Don't panic, I'm coming back.

Sorry the bananas I sent were all dried up and glad that the last lot of lemons were in good condition. I'd so banked on you having a treat. Two letters from home and one from Jack and Mrs A. and understand you've been over on a visit. Will you tell me if Dad's illness is a passing phase or serious and likely to be fatal. So please tell me as your trained mind sees it, as I cannot feel at ease until I know. Each day is getting cooler and the nights have a definite chill. Our moves are in the right direction and under canvas again. The journey up here quite comfortable. The inhabitants are getting in the last grapes. Oh to see the English countryside again! That's all. Bless you, N.

21 October 1943

Must apologise for the writing papers – it belongs 'the Firm'. Thanks for your very sweet letters. I repeatedly re-read them. The men are still suffering septic sores. Only about one tenth not affected. The cleaning and duration take such a long time. We are short of fresh vegetables and vitamins. We have very little bread and too much tinned food and after all the heat, filth and living conditions, I've had such ghastly sores and ulcers go wrong. Burns immediately do. Can you get me a couple of thermometers. The only one I had got broken and I need the use of one for the many cases of colds and tonsilitis. Whilst on the subject of need, will you send at the same time shaving cream, Macleans and Brylcream, which would be acceptable as a Christmas present. No allowance is made for being unshaven whatever the circumstances.

Yes, there is an African Star. The Germans and Italians seem to be well medalled and ribboned. Personally I'd prefer a few bob, nay a few quids instead!

Thanks for explaining about my Dad, dear, and I have a feeling he won't get better from this lot. I understand – I'm bound to look at it in this light as he is getting old and cannot stand much more, but I'd like to see him again, as he would me. Do what you can, dear.

I'm gradually getting nearer you. My love is as great and constant to you as it ever was. It is seven months since last I saw you. I do revel in reading your mail so very many times. Sorry I cannot help repeating this. Gradually getting back to you, I'm perfectly fit and as happy and comfortable as I can be. As always, N.

Air Mail   29 October 1943

There's a bundle of mail from you to answer and I must get down to a decent ordinary letter as soon as possible. About the incoming mail, the last one took only twelve days. I've had a lad in from another section and took him off to hospital with a high temperature, head and body ache, having a rigor and dry lung, so that was a two hour job. I cannot attempt to answer all you tell me so I will only touch on the latest so that we keep up to date. The mail is reaching us with the minimum delay. It indicates that we could move on. So the Ivesons have come back to life – thought they would somehow, etc, etc.

Wish I'd never mentioned them; the very name 'Ken' always sparked off a revolt. Myself I never had an enduring jealousy and they were my friends of long-standing. Remembering at my place of work, where by this time the elderly men and younger were in reserved occupation, (to fill the need of supplying steel), and these 'certain types' had to be thwarted. I managed them. Thank God I kept it to myself.

Air Graph   2 November 1943

My last letter to you was an air mail and I am trying, though doubt if I'll succeed in answering the considerable mail. We have no special news and like your air graphs to me are only a stop-gap. I know you will understand. The parcels we send have to have the contents quoted and signed, priced and such. Haven't received anything from the comforts fund you mentioned as yet. Love, N.

Green Letter   4 November 1943

Just been having a good wash down and feel better for it. I had a postal order from the comforts fund. A letter from Mum repeats how good you and Wing have been to her. I've sent off to Ken and Ivy as I'd had a letter from them. Ivy speaks in glowing terms of her love for me! A letter home to Mum and Dad after being out all day going back to Foggia. I seem to have a bigger 'practice' than a Harley Street specialist. I get babes in arms with tummy-ache and old grandpas with gout and at all hours of the day. Kiddies jabbering like monkeys; some are really great. Another six months and I'll be able to speak fluent Italian and the kiddies, English. I've had some rotten little accidents to attend. The main problem is that the families are too big to rear properly and the kiddies get into a lot of mischief. I had three cases of burns one afternoon, through lighting explosives. Poor little beggars, in such shock and pain, but I shipped them off to hospital. Only one came back who I'm treating and he's nearly cured. I thought he was deaf until today when he said 'Grazia'. I've also had a little lad in with a finger end off. He did howl – so another off to the hospital. No dear, if you bang a drum long and hard enough someone will notice, but if you sit and gently play the violin the world goes by. Have you hidden depths of talents I don't know of? I think if you went on stage and told the story of your mother's specs, it would bring the house down.

I appreciate the parcel with all the toiletries including toothbrush. It had taken five and a half weeks. Today may mark another great phase in this bloody war. The Russians advance, but slowly. The great four meet in Tehran. We are on the move this side of the 'leg'. The American Fifth have started their advance and our bombing policy is still assuming gigantic proportions and yet to come out of the bag are the armies of Jumbo Wilson and Mountbatten. All I guess ready and waiting, to say nothing of the Yanks and Canacks and our boys of England. Be prepared for a bloody Christmas and New Year – but a new year of hope and victory, so be thankful, my dear, for the continual health, strength and fortitude, all of which are needed for the women who wait. Thinking of you at all possible times. N.

Little did he know that, but have been able to show repartee, jokes and acting in a small way and still continue. Like the bus conductor who said 'Plenty of seats upstairs, Missis', so I said 'Well fetch me one down then!' Sorry I had to say it.

Air Mail   8 November 1943

Have been very neglectful of late and it's a week since sending you a graph. Each night I'm trying to put Christmas messages on graphs, both for my friends and other chaps and I'm now stalled. I've chucked the one I was trying to do for you, as I don't think I can do you credit. We have tried to purchase the real ones with no luck. Your mail of 21 September is the last one I've had. The post has just arrived and there's an air mail from Mum in which she says Dad is still in bed in the same condition and I'm afraid it is getting her down. I'm sorry in each of her letters she seems to be up against it. So hope Dad soon shows some improvement. No news, same as before. Keep smiling. Tons of love, N.

Air Mail   10 November 1943

Had your letter and one from Mum today, both of which were very beautiful and made me so very pleased that I have a mother and wife like you both at a time like this. Thank you, Sweetheart, for your sympathy and all you have done for Mum. My dad, like me, fell in love with you from our first meeting. He even met you before I did and at all times thought highly of you, both as a woman and in your professional capacity. I do grieve a little and cannot help it, though trying not to. You see he worshipped me and carried me miles and miles when a kid and went all over the place when I ran in competitions and played representative football and took pride in everything I did. When I became a tradesman I was the only joiner in the world! I'm only sorry I couldn't be there when he went away. To close, dear, my OC, to whom you so thoughtfully wrote, has written a reply on the next page and interviewed me this evening. I cannot think at this moment of anything I want doing. Major Laird has given me this mail and one for Mum. I'm all right, dear, don't worry and I will write more when I get another ordinary letter. N.

Enclosure

Dear Mrs Bell

Thank you so much for your letter card today, telling me of the death of your father-in-law. I have spoken to your husband and given what sympathy I can, but there is so little one can do to soften the blow. I can assure you of my depth of sympathy as my own father died when I was in France early in the war. Thank you for your wishes, I can only hope that it is not so long before this war is over and we can start living our lives again.

Yours very sincerely

Martin Laird

Air Graph   13 November 1943

Your mail of 27 October made no mention of Dad's health and yours of the 4th of this month telling me of his funeral. Glad the sun shone, I do wish I could have been there to help Mum. Thanks for your help to her. Dad was very upset when I last saw him and he trembled with emotion and a tear in his eye. I'm leaving any advice as regards Mum to you. I'm OK, Dear, don't worry. My love, N.

Sorry to continue what may seen a morbid period to you. Fortunately, I was able to arrive for the funeral, which had been arranged for me to get there in time by train. Strangely I was somewhat horrified when I opened the sitting room door and behind was the coffin. Nobody told me Dad was there while Aunt Loui, Mum's sister was preparing a cold lunch of Spam and beetroot. How I pushed it down remains with me still. Then when two horses and a bier arrived I was thrown again, but this

*was country method and the 'in thing' in the area apparently
and we walked behind on the way to church. Children danced
around us on our way, as if in some sort of a circus. Mum was
getting old and I don't know how she did it. I felt weak limbed.
I continued spending many of my monthly weekends off with
her. She was able to now have a 'bank book' with what was
left from the insurance after paying the funeral fee. Like today
some have plenty some not.*

Green Letter   15 November 1943

I don't know how long this letter will be, as I believe we're
moving tomorrow. I'll try and keep a line of thought as I'm
inclined to jump about a bit. Yes, we have been near Mount
Etna. She loomed above us, hidden by cloud and smoke all
day long, but had on one side the deepest purple in shadow,
but that was ages ago. Now we are up on the Adriatic Coast,
the blue of the sea changing to green and looking very cold.
So you've finally got some decent lemons. It's a wonder, for
the box they were packed in was a poor effort.

I never knew my Mother when she was young, she was
thirty-fivish and Dad fiftyish when I was born. I do know she
was a beautiful woman, her devotion to me excelled by my
Dad. His outlook was of an older period. I'm afraid their
devotion to me made me the conceited pig I am today. Take
care, enjoy life. All love, N.

*Fifty years on, previous boxed gifts to me are still in use in my
sewing drawer and the contents given on the outside still legible,
such as 2lbs currants, 2lbs sultanas.*

132

Air Mail   19 November 1943

We have been moving again. This entails preparing, loading and setting up new premises. This place is colossal. Pigs, chickens and horses almost eat off the same table as the people do, even their ablutions together. It's a case of putting the pig to bed and if there's any room left, get in yourself. We ourselves have decent billets, so all's well and just about straight and in order. Since tea I've had a personal clean up. It being my birthday, my celebration is a bottle of beer and big congratulations from two mates, Stan the cobbler and Maurice the ration corporal. Have had loads of newspapers but no letter from you for over a week. All my love, N.

Air Mail   28 November 1943

Sunday afternoon and although finished work, most likely will get interruptions. I've just had to issue a pair of shoes. Have had letters of 11, 15 and 16 October from you and many letters from others to answer, but my concern is for you and Mum. Please find out what's the matter with the foot she complains of. I will find it difficult to answer Ivy's letter, it's so heart-rending. Will be with you again soon. I'm all right. Bye, N.

Air Mail   6 December 1943

Have sent off an air graph as a Xmas greeting the last day of posting to the UK. My mail from you sadly lacking, had nothing for ten days. The parcel you last sent arrived in the nick of time with only three days of shaving cream left. We've had good weather, which collapsed today, which is foggy, drizzly and awfully grey, just like our back-end English weather. Remember our long walks together in wind and rain, returning to a glowing fire with a healthy appetite?

133

The news tonight is of the Tehran conference, so have great hopes of the outcome. Nothing to report. If you listen to the wireless news you will know as much as me, but I'm full of confidence for our future. I've heard Percy B. has died. So sad, he and Mrs B. were so kind to us. My very best wishes to you for Xmas. Have a happy time and that in the coming New Year our hopes will be realised. Bye dear, N.

Air Graph   10 December 1943

Just had your letter of 23 November, making it ten days again since hearing from you. Surely you must be writing more regularly than ten days. Mind you, last Wednesday I received the song book and it's smashing, just the job. In fact the three of us have been at it already. All I want now is a similar copy of this last year's number. Yesterday I received a parcel from Mum and Dad, posted three days before he died. It contained the same as yours and a fountain pen. It appears to have taken six weeks in reaching me. I've had a letter from Bailey who's in dock in Africa and a graph from Edith and Syd, still in civvy street. All my love, N.

Green Letter   13 December 1943

My last letter to you was a very poor graph as your mail had been few and far between. Your next letter took only five days. Johnny Hoare is back with us again and has dysentery. I cannot believe that Mum manages on her income and I rely on you to be judge of her need. So what you say makes me happier. I think her usual cheerful self will take charge. It's my belief also that you have had something to do with her not going out to work. I'm assured once again that you have been a godsend to her. I promise I won't forget it and will try to make up for what you have done.

Thanks for young Ken's address. It would be grand to find him, should he be in a near locality. I've been out with a truck today. The roads were so crowded, it took us nine hours to get there and back. Have had a smashing tea of fresh fish, tinned peas, bread and spread, (can't call it butter). Not being far from the coast we get fish about twice a week – small ones like haddock and very tasty. We get on quite well with the locals. It is remarkable that they turn out so clean. Shoes and boots are few and far between. Normally they wear wood soles with a bit of material round the big toe. No stockings, frocks and skirts very short and often shabby. The elderly wear shawls. On festival days or general holiday, come what may, war or no war, they turn out in smashing array. Coloured handkerchiefs cover curly hair, spotlessly clean dresses and lovely stockings, cheeky shoes with very high heels. When I see them cleaning out pigs in a morning on hands and knees and looking like a bill-stickers bucket, well it puts me off and makes me thankful to own somebody of a hundred per cent back in England. You will be getting several more mails before you receive this. Bye my dear, N.

Air Mail   14 and 19 December 1943

As usual I am going through one of my impatient periods of waiting for letters from you. Mum's letter seemed as if she didn't quite know what to think of Ivy and Ken Iveson when you both went to tea. Expect they were rather explosive and voluble. She wouldn't understand them and didn't quite get it at all. Mum says flu is rampant, so take care. Lemons and almonds are on the way to you. Had your letter of 5th December. No more news this end. All love, N.

I still have one almond in my purse after fifty years.

Air Mail   24 December 1943

Christmas and I want to be with you for a few minutes before
I go out. We are asked out for a meal at 8 p.m. Had your
letters of 10th December, then one for the November 15th
with photo of Mum and you. You both look as I remember
you. Bless you both and thanks a lot. I've also had your
beautiful Xmas card – so like you. Your Xmas parcel from
me was sent in October, amongst which was one pair of silk
stockings to replace the ones damaged whilst assisting at that
accident and because of your coupon shortage. I'm with you
in mind. Keep smiling and all love to you. N.

Green Letter   29 December 1943

So you have snow. Here it is bitterly cold and the sky full.
The mountains are covered in snow. We've had cloud, cold
winds and fitful sunshine. We'll soon have to wear vest and
pants. Hope to hear from you soon and find that you have
received the parcel. It gave me such pleasure to choose the
contents. It's funny how similar things happen to you and
me. I've noticed it scores of times. I too had part of a tame
rabbit for supper the other night with the folks across the
road and the skin was drying over the door. It was a big white
one, or bianco as the Italians say. By the way, we had turkey
at the Xmas Eve supper I mentioned previously. It followed
soup and very good too and several other dishes and the most
delicious pastries. I cannot imagine how they are able to cook
them as it's only a hearth oven with wood that they gather
for free. Later we sat drinking their wine and our whisky until
1.00 a.m. No I didn't get drunk either then or over Xmas.
Minimum work on Xmas day, no parades and only duties
strictly necessary. I helped rig up the big workshop for the
concert and ate sparingly for dinner as we later played football,
or tried, on a ploughed field. I had the doubtful privilege of
kicking the ball through my own goal. I said it was the goalie's

fault, but have no doubt it was mine. After football, I showered and had dinner. What a spread – roast pork (we bought a pig), turkey, apple sauce, roast and boiled potatoes, tinned peas and lovely gravy. Then Xmas pudding and custard, wine and two bottles of beer. Maurice, Stan and I had a lie down till 7.00 p.m. and then went to the concert. We had a lad with an Italian band, the rest very good in an improvised way – army style. Come the interval there were nuts, oranges and figs, and several kinds of pastries, made by our own cooks. Also tea, coffee and wine. We finished about 10.30 p.m. Bed didn't come early as we had enforced guests who drank rather deeply. Boxing Day was work as usual and the same kind of dinner as previous. Now, however, we are back to normal. Systems are beginning to function normally and headaches diminishing. Though by some of the antics and appearances of some of our lads, doubt if they'll get back to normal again!

The locals are a most callous lot in killing their pet pigs, which have lived with them almost as humans. Then, women and children crowd round and hold the pig whilst someone sticks the pig and seem to derive some satisfaction from seeing its gore all over the place. Blood on roads, buildings and kids and yet they themselves cannot stand a mere scratch, and I mean scratch, and expect to be a stretcher case. That's the menfolk. The women seen to be able to stand more and are certainly by far the most hysterical.

I have an air mail to send you tonight which will get to you ages before this. Writing these private letters gives me the most enjoyment, the nearest I can get talking to you with privacy intact. Ten months have passed since leaving our homeland. How much longer? Bye my love, N.

Air Mail   30 December 1943

Like a ray of sunshine I received your letter of the 16th which
tells me that you have finally received the Xmas parcel. My
joy and relief when I read this, as I thought it had gone West
and if Mum's got hers I'm in heaven! Johnny H. was here
for Xmas day. Bailey still way back in hospital. Curry is here
too. Our weather is cold with sunny spells about midday. The
locals say they get snow in January. I'm not looking forward
to it. Have had quite a number of *Daily Mails* and a parcel
of 200 cigarettes which arrived at the same time – I've
acknowledged them. Had a nice letter from Bert W. and
sympathy about Dad. Good news of the war at present. Let's
hope the good news continues. Yours, N.

Air Mail   3 January 1944

This is my first letter to you in this New Year. All the best
that is possible to you. Sunny days, happy dreams and the
longing to be with you. Had your letter of 7 November on 1
January. I know you are maintaining regular letters and they
are getting through by delay and haphazardly, the continuity
hit and miss. I've been particularly busy with new arrivals
and all over the place getting in stores. We finished off the
old year with a film show, *Slightly Dangerous*, reminding me
of what I was missing. After we had a smashing dinner at
8.30 p.m. when we sang and drank until 12.00 a.m., finishing
with Auld Lang Syne. Much hand-shaking and off to bed,
and I still didn't get drunk.

New Year's Day was terribly terribly cold and a snorting
gale even washed a ship ashore. Have had a letter from Curry's
wife. All the best to start a New Year. Deep love, N.

N. was a moderate drinker. Only once did I see him near the borderline. He seemed so happy I refrained from hitting him. That was in civvy street. He enjoyed a pint in the British Legion Club, which was built of part brick and part wood. I did get a notion to put a match to it! Later when we ran our own business it was a form of relaxation and he enjoyed being amongst menfolk.

Air Mail   8 January 1944

Have had your letter today of 28 December, our anniversary. I see we were both occupied at the same time. It's remarkable how we seem to be doing the same thing at the same time. Glad you found the stockings were good ones. All the troops are pouncing on them. I believe all the army postal services are dealt with by the Royal Engineers, if interested. Expect I'll get an ordinary letter off to you in February. We get spells of sunshine and the local ladies sit out in the sun, knitting and jabbering, escaping from the kids and pigs for a while. Had a little excitement when one of their stables set on fire. The donkey went west, and the pigs have all been killed and their squeals are no more. Take care, be with you soon. With love, N.

Green Letter   9 January 1944

Managed this ordinary letter. Glad you got the bungalow. I'm afraid I was a bit short-sighted in why you felt the need of one. So you opened your parcel before Xmas. We were only allowed to send goods to the value of 30s. (£1.50). We are at a place that has been very much in the news lately, which is now our main base. The roads are terrible and don't half get a bashing with thousands of tanks, trucks and cars running over them twenty four hours a day and every day. We have a periodical burst of rumours and at its height just now. We cannot believe any of them, some are awful to contemplate. Generally there is a spark of truth at the bottom of it. By the time you get this, we will have moved elsewhere. Monty is in England for what might be another great push or event. We've had foul weather and tearing winds. Our bombers and fighters fill the sky – it is still war. Bye love, N.

Air Graph   14 January 1944

There's no mail from you and I haven't much to say and a graph doesn't take much filling. My thoughts have been with 'Hideaway' and how you're faring with it. I feel we are wasting our lives together. There seems no end to this situation. Although I moan, some of the lads out here haven't been home for three, four and five years. We had one leave for England after six years of foreign service. In Mum's letter she tells me that her Xmas parcel hasn't arrived yet. Reckon must write it off as finished. Thats all, dear. All love, N.

Green Letter   30 January 1944

Down in the valley everything is quite fertile and the land nearly all cultivated and strange to say still has clusters of cacti and various vegetables I've not seen before. Corn and beans are growing where the war has passed and grape vines undergoing their pruning. Patterned rows of diamond and wigwam shapes. There are birds in abundance, sparrows and wrens. There's even a patch of grass here and there – an uncommon sight since leaving England.

Sheep, goats and pigs have diminished but there are horses, donkeys and mules and large white bullocks working all over the place. The locals even have cows yoked in carts from which they get milk in small amounts. I've never seen any herd grazing yet. The locals are poor specimens. How Musso dare venture into war has me frazzled. It's obvious that these poor beggars have never enjoyed prosperity any more than they do now. Every building is in ruins and there are few main roads. The locals seem to do a lot of interbreeding. I've admired the ladies' good looks and figures until childbirth seems to change their attractiveness. There is filth and dirt, kids and lice, no housing or property that's up to standard.

This has been a very long move and we are expecting to move on a few more miles tomorrow. Our big move took us over mountain after mountain, and up incredible twisting roads. Twas bitterly cold at night. A fleet of new trucks had burnt out their brakes the day before we left.

It's a case of scribbling when I can. Our food is good, the cooks do us well. We get fresh meat almost every day and beautiful cauliflowers. Having accumulated some good soup stock, had it for tea last night. We have had some fresh smoked back bacon sometimes for breakfast and tea and white bread. Bailey is still in dock in Algiers.

I'd just put page 7 at the top and 1.2.44 when we had to load up in earnest. Our move took us ten miles. Still under canvas in a field under trees and been able to convert a big room for recreation, with light and heat, writing and games tables. I've met a corporal here from Gypsyville (in Hull) and he has not been home for four years. He isn't very happy about it, but we both felt better after talking about Hull City Rovers and the fair and all the beer we were going to drink when we did get back.

3 February 1944

Last night was my turn to visit an ENSA show, which was smashing. The continuity of the acts like clockwork. Love as always, N.

Green Letter 13 February 1944

I'd be obliged if you will excuse me should I make a miserable effort and moan and groan. I'll try not to. The weather is lousy with torrential rain, hail and howling winds, everywhere a sea of mud and leaking canvas and beds wet. By the time you receive this, we could be basking in sunshine. I've been a duck for weeks. I have had issued by the NAAFI one Italian razor blade and it carries a woman's face as an advert! Your letters to hand of 23 and 30 January. Jerry has retired to better positions and has fought every inch of the way. There are signs of war everywhere.

I have not been out since our arrival. The only locals are those working for us and a few women who come and collect and wash our laundry. Animals and food are very short, terribly in fact. Life isn't very funny for them. Some places are completely wiped out, there are heaps of rubble through which bulldozers have pushed a road for transport. A scene of bitter fighting. Don't worry about me, the front has moved on – life according to routine orders. I'm not a big strong soldier in the thick of it and not in the new landing.

14 February 1944

I've sent off to you a rather patchy air mail. We are having to get accustomed to freezing nights and cold after Africa. How long it seems now. Although I haven't had the chance of seeing it, there's a show on for three days with Leslie Henson Kenway and Young. So bet it will be a smasher. Once in a blue moon these occasions help tremendously. Our fighting is still pretty bloody and some of our companion companies have been in it. I know a couple of our lads got a packet and hope they come out of it OK. I have been out of camp today in a jeep to ordnance for stuff and got a glorious view of range after range of snow-covered mountains and jagged outcrops

142

of flowing grandeur, shaded from pure white to many greys with purple shadow in the depth. Across the lot were staggering splashes of golden sunshine. But one cannot forget the war and I came back to earth as we slid past convoys of supplies going up and forever moving on, clanking and groaning with vibrations and then a shower unit just round a mountain bend and a line of glistening bodies freshening up. That's all, dear heart, there'll come a day of reunion. N.

Air Mail   18 February 1944

Letters from you seem to be getting through quicker. Thanks for looking out for the thermometers. I know these things are difficult to get just now. The 'M' you mention reminds me of a ruddy fish just dying but can't manage it and snappy every few minutes. Is she subject to pity or a nuisance? Get off and have this wacking holiday with Jessie. Wish it was me. All for now. Much love, N.

Air Graph   23 February 1944

Your air mails of the 7th, 10th and 15th of this month have made good time. I am at last a recognised joiner in the army, my trade rating having come through from England. It doesn't mean an increase in pay. The smudges on this paper are caused by raindrops, as it's pouring again. We had a debate on post-war England this afternoon. That's all, with love, N.

Green Letter   3 March 1944

The rain has been pelting down now for weeks, so you can imagine the quagmire. Occasionally we get odd hours of glorious sunshine. Some say it is a rainy month in this region and it has started well and truly. I'm told also that next month will be sunshine and hot weather. No mail now for fifteen days – my biggest moan and I'm longing to hear from you and don't place the blame with you.

Remember how I've raved about my trade and not having touched any tools for eleven months and was known as a pioneer sapper. Joiners are graded 'B'. I'd applied in the beginning for joinery. Our second in command, whom I get on with, asked if I wished to start up in my trade – imagine what I said – with fifteen years experience behind me, I'd like to have been awkward but I knew I'd be happier with my old job. I said that I'd like to get to the top grade and would like to go into the technical section he had offered and work alongside the other joiner, as two were needed. My new mate, who I get on well with, is George Harvison who comes from Lincolnshire. He's a tradesman on top rate of pay, getting 7s. 6d. ($37\frac{1}{2}$p) a day. I'm hoping to get better grading and pay soon and hoping too that medical duties will be taken off me. A laddie in our class was posted to another company after becoming an NCO and has lost an eye and leg whilst clearing mines. If you decide to go without food if my mail doesn't arrive, then I think I'll decide to stay in bed if none arrives from you tomorrow!

Thirty one is a big age as my grandfather used to say, so when I do come home I hope there's no wrinkles or that you are wearing red flannel abb wool or a truss! Whilst I am losing hair, have flat feet, varicose veins and my knees are getting knobbly.

Our NAAFI issues vary as weeks go by and we had no beer, chocolate or razor blades, but just now we've been issued with one bottle of Canadian beer, a bar of chocolate, chewing gum, razor blade, box of matches, thirty large Woodbines and forty Gold Flake – all for 40 lira. For the first time we've had mutton, well it could be lamb or ram, but it tasted good with

144

Yorkshire pudding and beans, which were hard, and then unsweetened rice pudding. Funny how there's generally something wrong with a meal and if you can manage to stand upright in the mud as you try and find a seat. You dream of the cooking you left behind. All love, N.

Air Mail   9 March 1944

I've had some mail from you of 9th, 21st and 29th February. So you have snow at last. Wish I was with you to go tobogganing. Remember our spills and thrills?

Glad you got the nuts and oranges I sent. Mum says she got hers too. It's a year last Sunday since we said goodbye. I have plenty of work and enjoying it. All love, N.

I remember well this period of heavy snow and cold and the embarrassment when my sister-in-law told me, though delicately, that I had an icicle on my nose-end! How long I'd had it I do not know as I stood for ages in a queue feeling numb and perished waiting for bread.

Air Graph   14 March 1944

Since writing to you last I have piles of mail from you, along with music copies and *Picture Post*. We have seen another show with a dance band of the RASC. Very good too. Have had to have a tooth out, it was pretty rotten. I've had two parcels from Mum, solidly packed and John Bulls all over the place. We had just left the Old Country a year ago. That's all sweetheart, N.

Green Letter

22 March 1944

I'm attempting to answer your letters to hand, including that great long beauty of 16 January. The Americans are here in this area; therefore the odds and ends I like to send you have gone up in price and the Italians are making a mint.

I see very little of the enemy and if anything is going on I don't see it as Death and Glory, just the terrific amazement of it all. I have recollections of 109s coming over in Africa and Sicily and of me shouting like hell as the ack-ack chased them away. I had to give them a good old English soldier's cursing.

I could do with a nail file, dear, and the usual pot of shaving cream. Your little parcel of toothpaste and thermometers arrived two days ago and if I finish with medical duties they are still useful. I feel heartbroken that you haven't yet had your birthday parcel. Might as well tell you that it is a swimsuit. I have just read a satire on militarism by Paul Marche, called *Fools Like Me*. It's a smashing read. We have been stationary this last nine weeks. I've no idea but feel there's more pending and can't think we'll be leaving this country yet.

Did I tell you I had the lucky experience of seeing Vesuvius in eruption? White-hot larva a quarter of a mile wide engulfing villages. A most majestic column of smoke imaginable, with ashes falling miles away. It was impossible to look up and trucks with headlights on in the middle of day. Roofs were caving in under the weight and bulldozers were clearing the streets. Should there be a gap in my mail, you will know why. Bye Bye love, N.

146

Air Graph   2 April 1944

I've had a batch of *Picture Post* from you, but no letters. You will see by the date it is Palm Sunday and it's a most beautiful day. We are having one of those few half-days, so doing all my odd jobs and then an hour's ease before tea. Then there's football to wind up the day. I feel a book is in order and I'm reading *Madam Claire* by Susan Ertz, a Penguin book. It's a restful and pleasing type. Work proceeds as usual and all is OK – if things carry on as now. Hope to write again soon. All love, N.

Air Mail   7 April 1944

It's Good Friday evening and there's pork for dinner, no fish. Hope we get more pork. Our weather is now gloriously hot. In a day or two it will be like Africa. We haven't the desert to contend with but the roads are pure dust. I hope the better weather doesn't bring its batch of illnesses again. It's been like heaven to be free again over the winter period. The mosquito seems to be coming into its own again and nets will soon be in use.

We have moved on again, dear, and are camped on the terraced side of the mountains. A lovely spot amongst vines and olive trees and we look right across a valley. Hope your spring-like weather continues. I have vivid memories of very cold Easters. I'm rather elated that the beech trees are down, or so I hear, but waiting confirmation from you. We have a wireless loud speaker extension in the trees and in the central building, so we heard Churchill's speech and are able to get most good programmes. I was on guard last night. The moonlight was beautiful and it was warm too. I could see for miles. The bullfrogs were croaking away and occasionally I could hear owls calling. I've had another letter from Winko at Naples – do wish I could see him. That's all my love. N.

Air Mail   12 April 1944

Mail is scarce again, so I'm looking forward to a good post one day soon. This is the most lovely campsite with a few old oak trees and a type of holly all around. Whilst on guard the other night I enjoyed the song of the nightingale for about two hours in the moonlight. We like this place a lot, even though we are besieged with women and children at meal times, begging for scraps, rather pitiful. I cannot forecast the end of this war, so do keep happy and smiling as I've always known you. My health is fine and manage a game of football now and again. Just plan for when I get back. You are never far away in my mind. My love to you, N.

Air Graph   16 April 1944

Have had mail from you of 25 March, 2, 3 and 10 April. Your news that the trees are really down cheered me up. I think I have been worrying about that needlessly. The weather is hotting up and with a goodly tan I kid myself that I look like Adonis or a half-baked swaddy! Although this is a glorious place, and you would revel in it, it is marred by wire slit trenches and all other signs of warfare. There are kiddies in abundance dressed in rags and in a most revolting filthy state. The poverty cannot be described and they hang around at meal times. I have been lifted a grade so I'm rather fussy my work has been noticed and enjoying it and been congratulated on it. A book I'm reading is another of Susan Ertz's, *Now East Now West*. I've already read *The Scarlet Pimpernel*, must be the tenth time. Laying awake I sometimes remember going over miles of countryside when I was a boy. Ever yours, N.

Air Graph   26 April 1944

Your letter of the 16th arrived tonight to cheer me up after a pouring wet day and mud everywhere. I have come back from two days rest, a lazy time. Saw a show and two films and had a cup of tea in bed as a highlight. We won 3-0 tonight at football, playing in a knockout competition, the strongest teams to form an Eighth Army league. We won 4-1. It's almost overpoweringly hot, but I'm liking it so far. We're now up to the eyes in work, even to be on shifts. You ask if I need anything. Well I could do with some lemon crystals and a pair of brown stockings. All love, N.

Air Graph   6 May 1944

I'm afraid it's only a graph this time and won't be able to manage much in reply to yours of 22 April. Incidentally, I can do with a mail from you soon. Your photo hasn't arrived yet, nor the ordinary mail after your visit to Mum. So waiting for both keenly. This will be a disappointment to you.

Just a little information in passing. We get a daily paper called the *Union Jack* and a weekly *Crusader*. I'll enclose one or the other in an ordinary letter sometime. Americans have *Stars and Stripes*, Canadians a *Maple Leaf*, Aussies, New Zealanders and South Africans have one I believe. It's a single sheet used on both sides and very good. There'll be a cutting also from a Sunday paper of Inga Anderson I once told you about. I didn't think she would be allowed to sing songs to you that she did for us. We have been issued with a beret less a pom-pom. That's it with all love, N.

Two very scrappy graphs and an ordinary green letter with previously mentioned cutting and papers arrived for May. Very evasive and lacking in substance until:

Air Mail   3 June 1944

I've a confession to make and will tell you the truth. I'm in
dock between sheets in bed, it's lovely. I'd heard so much
about it thought I'd try it. Yes, a cosy bed, really delicious
food and beautiful nursing sisters. (More about those another
time). No I'm not dying, it isn't VD but a common complaint
out here – jaundice. I have felt ill for weeks, but not enough
to go sick. In the end they made me go. I talked myself out
on light duty after a week. (The time you were on holiday).
I've been sent back right away to a big hospital again and
may get sent further back to a hospital near Naples. Keep on
writing as before to the company and do not worry. I'll write
and inform as to progress. My love to you, N.

Air Mail   14 June 1944

According to my regular habits, I should have written to you
yesterday, but it was the CO's inspection and consequently
didn't have our daily overhaul by the MO. Therefore, I
thought it better to wait until he had been today and was
able to tell you anything that was going on. I'm glad I did
for I'm to report to a convalescent depot in the near future.
Tomorrow I presume I'll be off after getting my discharge etc.,
and away by the Friday the 16th. I'm not sure if I mentioned
that I've made a mate of a Leeds lad, but we're both in with
the same thing and been in together all the time and going
out together, so it isn't so bad. I don't relish all the movement.
I'd much prefer to go back to the company but the MO won't
hear of it. He says if I don't take it steady I'll be back with
a second and worse dose. So there it is.

I have your letter of 21 May when you were on holiday. I
do hope you enjoyed every minute, even the twenty mile hike.
The war is still moving and by the time you get this letter it
will have marched on a few miles more. I'd like to think I

150

could get back to my unit. Just to close, I'm still thinking of you at all hours and wish I could see your smiling eyes, which I remember every time a sister wanders by, but I only make myself miserable and sad thinking of you and how sublimely happy we surely were. It's a beautiful thought. Don't worry. Love, N.

Air Mail   18 June 1944

It's Sunday morning and we haven't a duty of any kind, not even a check parade. There has been a voluntary church service but I'm too lazy and so far since breakfast have only managed to stagger over to the NAAFI for a drink of tea and cake. That being the only excursion expended with the exception, of course, of that ever present past-time of killing bloody flies! Yesterday we had an inspection by the dental officer, were graded by the MO, had a lecture on VD by the CO and a talk by the padre and that was it. Last night we had a concert by an ENSA party and it was smashing. It was very hot. What with flies, mosquitoes and VD, this country is nearly as bad as Africa.

Tomorrow I start light PT, whatever that may be, and I only expect being here a week or ten days and then I start on the road back and what a job that will be. This place, dear, is a new Italian barracks, a bit knocked about but not bad. We sleep on stretchers, have good food and not much work. We are allowed out each day after 5.00 p.m. and Saturdays after 2.00 p.m. and Sundays after 11.00 a.m. In all cases we have to be in by 9.00 p.m. By the above you will see I haven't anything to complain about, but I don't feel settled. One lacks privacy, etc. There are over 3000 men of the British regiments getting better after sickness, accidents and wounds. I want badly to get back to the few in my company, if I can't get back to you. This is the convalescent depot and it's only a few miles from the hospital. I must try to visit the city.

151

Incidentally, quite near to where I purchased your swimsuit. Don't worry your sweet head. Bye my love, N.

Air Mail 29 June 1944

At last I'm back with the boys and happy once again. Thanks dearest for all your mail waiting for me. Seven in all, the last one being 20 June. I had four from Mum, one from Edith and Syd, one from young Ken and ordinaries from Arthur Bailey, Bert W. and Mrs H. with 10s. (50p) from the comfort fund, and an ordinary from Wing. I think I'd better just tell you of my happenings and leave yours until next time and may not get all in one mail. I also want to apologise for not having written you before this – it's eleven days since my last. I managed to talk myself out of the convalescent camp after a week. Then my troubles started for I had to go to a transit camp and then make my way across to this side again by road, along with about a hundred vehicles. Ours, unfortunately, turned out a dud and what with being short of food, water and petrol, we were in a bonny mess. However, we struggled on washing and drinking in rivers and eating fruit from the trees and buying it and eggs in the villages, begging petrol from odd passing trucks. For we were on a very secondary route and with the use of much bad language, we eventually got to our destination. Here I buggered off. I'd had enough and in so doing I have laid myself open to a charge of desertion, for I'd gone against the all-godly rules and regulations. But whatever happens, I can say I was back within a day with my unit. If I'd stopped and been herded back by the powers that be, it would have taken a couple of months. However, don't worry your sweet head, dear, but I believe the OC is on my side. So I think taking it all round I shan't get shot after all, but one never knows and it would be funny to become a corpse for getting back quicker than is usual. We swim in a beautiful headline river and life is good. That's all my love and heart, N.

Green Letter 2 July 1944

I wrote you an air mail two days ago and this is my next. I find I have much to answer since the pile I found waiting for me whilst in dock. The morning after my return found me hard at work again and ever since, and I'm glad to say I've had no ill effects. In general, we all feel fatigued mid-afternoon when it is so very hot. Our camp is partly under mixed oak, walnut and olive trees; the rest is in a narrow flat area, with a few vines and fruit trees following the river. There are mountains and hills towering away on each side as far as one can see. Range after range, all shell-scarred. Perpetual memorials to the futility of war. Alas, I'm afraid we'll never learn. The river in winter is quite wide and swift, but diminishes as all Italian rivers do in the dry season to a mere trickle on a bare rocky bed and ours at the 'bottom of the garden' is doing that. We have managed to dam it and retain about five feet. Just enough to cover our carcase and as we have a half-day have spent part lazing and sweating, then in the river cooling and think I'll have another do after this letter. I'd love to tell you the name of the place, but can't. Before long I expect we will be on the move again, where I've no idea, but it will be in the right direction.

To refer back to the transit camp, twenty drivers were called, each man to a truck, the rest of us as passengers, and proceeded to come back by convoy – getting man and materials wanted with the greatest possible speed and ease. Some of our trucks, (well four and the one I was in), developed problems, various minor ones due to newness and lack of running in. We had set off with one day's rations, no water or petrol and actually lived by our wits for three days, pinching, swopping, begging and buying eggs, cherries, plums, pears, apricots and wine to keep going. Drinking and washing in rivers and begging petrol from the few trucks that passed us and we on a second class route. The better, quicker routes kept exclusively for war materials proper. Eventually we got to our destination after four days instead of one long one. The country was magnifi-

153

cent, but so dusty and winding up the steepest of roads, then crawling down into the valley again, backing up and double locking round some hairpin bends nearly at an angle of 45°. It was terrific! I tried to see Wink O but got pipped and then off to the RE training battalion, where I was actually destined for. This didn't suit me, I'd been what seemed months in reaching the lads, so I just cleared off. Firstly I had something to eat, a wash and on going into the NAAFI ran slap bang into one of our lads. I stayed with him that night and came back here the next day. I was a bit shaky about reporting to the OC, but was received almost with open arms. It made a sensation when I disclosed what I'd done in taking the law into my own hands by getting back in five days and laying myself open again for desertion. The OC quite understood after I'd explained a bit and found it rather funny. I expect I'll be awarded punishment of some sort.

I meant to answer your letters but as usual found myself talking about me. Enclosed is a group photograph and a mixture of tradesmen of the RE's technical section. Will you get a couple of copies taken off and send one to my Mum? Can you notice all the African Stars proudly displayed? Still very hot here and we work in socks, boots and shorts with flies ever tormenting. George Harvison says he is going to visit us, even if it's only to tell you what a bad tempered husband you have! I'm off to the river, there's a female screaming on the wireless.

3 July 1944

Went to bed after my swim last night. Today is Monday and I hope to start well. Yes, dear, I am niggly with cash – I've had to be. So did I really buy you a tennis racquet?!?!

Your photo arrived and has knocked all the stuffing out of me. It brings home with such force just what I'm missing. The world could go to hell and I'd do without worldly goods, so long as I had you, but I have and you are my comfort. Thanks for the promised parcel. Mum's had just arrived with lemon essence, sugar and saccharin tablets. Your letters are such a help, dear, when one is feeling tired out, filthy and what the war throws out. Since being away from my unit my medical job has gone to another laddie. I'm not sorry. No definite sign of a move yet, but don't think it will be long as we are getting behind. All love, N.

I must make reference to George. He was apparently rescued from the sea at Algiers when his ship went down. He was in the same convoy as Norman and later they met and became joiners together. After the war George suffered what was thought to be 'nerves' and was out of work for some time. On later contact he came to help and work in my man's business. A lovely chap who seemed to suffer almost constant headaches. As time went on and his condition worsened, he was admitted to a Sheffield hospital for surgery to his head. Arriving carrying his attaché case, he eventually went home by stretcher and his death when it came was a great sadness to us.

Air Mail   12 July 1944

We have been on the move again. Well over 200 miles. It's impossible to get time to write to you at length. Arthur Bailey has just walked in after months away. He looks fit, has scars on his elbow from operations, said to have been cellulitis. He has a huge bundle of mail and seven parcels, so we should have a happy hour or two.

On our first day of moving we did ten hours and seventeen hours on the second day. That day we were on our own with the heavy workshops and after about fifteen miles we had our first accident. A colossal trailer broke loose on a hill, knocking a truck completely over into a ditch. We had one man trapped and eventually got the truck back and laddie out, with only a badly bruised leg. Later another truck with seven in it overturned and somersaulted down to the bottom. Four came out with abrasions, three in hospital but going on favourably. Our truck and trailer completed the run without mishap but by the end of the journey we were all in. All love, N.

Air Mail   17 July 1944

Haven't heard from you since being in this location. In fact it's fifteen days and I'm puzzled as Mum's Sunday letters get here regularly. It does take a bit of reckoning up. I've been able to bring all my correspondence up to date. My reading at the moment is Naomi Jacob's *Leopards and Spots*. I'd like to recommend Ethel Mannin's *Confessions and Impressions*. I wouldn't like to tell you what I thought about it though. We've had an occasional fire from cause unknown, the ground and everything is so snuff dry. My work, living and sleeping partner, George, is in dock with malaria, so imagine he will be in for a fair time. I wish him well. All for now and all love, N.

Air Mail   22 July 1944

After worrying you that I wasn't getting any mail from you, I have received three in three days, 9 July, then 2 and finally 12 – again a bit erratic. Glad you are getting some tennis in. Yes, you did tell me that you may be called up for military nursing, so keep me informed. Didn't get chance to get you anything in Rome, had thought of earrings. Yes, I'm fit, dear, a bit tired on guard last night and have been working twelve hours daily. The charge against me has fallen through. A letter from Curry's wife says they've had a share of the new bombs and, like you, worried about Johnny Hoare's wife. Johnny says his wife and kiddie have been evacuated, but doesn't know where. Thank your mum and dad for good wishes. After a deluge of one day it's hot again. That's all. All love, N.

At this point in time I was to have a disturbing few letters from my husband quoting lack of correspondence. He also enlarged on a bit of mischief which crept in from a close relative, though no name was mentioned. I sensed who it was. Living a life almost as a nun, I took exception and said my piece. He would not accept any explanation. I wasn't living it up here at home in his absence, he was the centrepiece of my life. Supporting him and his needs in every way I could. This unnecessary situation need never have arisen. I trusted him totally and he should have done so with me. It seemed there were two women fighting for first place in his life. Any flaw I had was to seem of grave magnitude. I knew the pressures he was going through and was sure his illnesses hadn't helped and recovery hadn't helped because he hadn't given them time to. Letters from Norman were indifferent for some time and I carried on as before. He was on the carpet for his outbursts. Well, his letters were censored and he had told me this himself. My weekends of what had been a duty on behalf of him were curtailed for some time and he would learn about that. I was confounded when he really blew his top, all out of proportion and we had two sad miserable hearts for some time.

Picking out oddments in further letters when we were more stable, N. goes on to say:

Have received your parcel with socks, file, salts (various) and cigarettes and now half way through one of yours. So many thanks. We have been snowed under with work and expect moving on a short way. Each move entails taking down, loading, travelling and the re-setting up of our own tents and all the workshops. Anyhow, we can't get much further up just yet.

To continue now an air graph I must reserve my air mails where possible. I have just got settled for the night after being on another move, again up at 4.00 a.m. No mail to answer from you as yet, nor anything from Mum. Bye dear, N.

Air Mail

It must be a fortnight since I heard from you, Mum the same. Hope the little bits I write keep us in touch. We are in the wilds again and have been for some time. I intend sending you a little present when I get into civilisation again. I'll have a word with Johnny Hoare and if his wife is unhappy you could ask her to stay with you. I like your suggestion. I'll be sending a postal order for £25. Take £5 and get yourself something, anything that tickles your fancy. All love, N.

Air Mail

An ordinary and three air graphs arrived from you. Johnny Hoare's wife and baby have gone to another of our mate's homes to stay with his wife, so everything is satisfactory. The socks are grand, dear, I'd omitted to mention it was the knee type I'd needed to wear with shoes and knee shorts. My mum sent me a long pair, both of which facts may not appeal to you at the moment or your sense of humour. I've tried to spare you as it were. Last week one of our lads lost a brother out here and the same day had word from his wife that she is packing him up. Today another laddie's wife has had a child. We have so much to rely on back home. I've had your ordinary mail of 1 October. Apart from a rotten hangover from inoculations I'm alright. I managed to get a wasp sting on my shoulder and ran amok until I ran out of breath. My mother's decision to marry this bloke is hers entirely, if she doesn't like to consult me that's all there is to it. Would it have helped if you had said 'yes' or 'no'? All love, N.

Air Mail   18 October 1944

I had quite a post bag yesterday, one from Mum and yours
of the 6th and 9th. By now you should have heard from me.
Quite fit and busy now we've moved into billets and they are
grand. The works are in a big sardine factory, good concrete
floors and white tiled walls. The only bogey is the battered
roof and as it rained yesterday it wasn't too pleasant at work
or for the fishy smell. The billets are in the outbuildings. The
officers just over the way and practically undamaged. I am a
boarder on the top floor with white distemper and trazzo tiles.

It's gratifying for you, I'm sure, to receive such a good
superannuation and our joint total makes good reading. I'm
afraid my total seems rather insignificant, never mind it can't
be helped. Thanks for the birthday present in lieu of my return.
You often ask if there's anything I need or want and I find
there's a couple of things if you can manage them. One a light
khaki tie the other any odd Oxos or Bovril for a warm drink
this winter. That's all this time, don't work too hard and be
happy. Yours as ever, N.

Air Mail   1 November 1944

We are well and truly dried out now and have spare clothes
to change into should we get another wet spell. The OC was
round today and asking if everything was OK with Mum.
Rather nice of him I thought, in his quiet way. Yes, the fall
of Rome is one step nearer home. That's past tense now and
further progress is going on. It's a year since Dad died. Brief
though this is, I love you still, N.

Air Mail   24 November 1944

Have heard from Mrs A. who says you look ill, so presumably one of you is wrong. I'm my usual self. My mates' favourite saying is 'Bell is only happy when grumbling.' So that sums me up! Seeing it's nearing Xmas and as you advise me not to torture myself, I will bear it in mind.

We have moved somewhat forward again and things are lively all the time, but we have bursts of this nature all the way. No, I don't expect you to commence manual labour on 'Hideaway', now or ever, but if you feel the urge to forward the job as much as possible, I have plenty for you to do. Cheerio, N.

I'd got to the stage of being under his power and standing to attention to read his letters. Had he noticed in my letters, everything was up to date, as per his request. I wasn't having a permanent holiday.

Air Mail   12 December 1944

Our weather is lousy. Nights are generally disturbed. We've had casualties in town. We are fine though, after experiencing Jerry's playfulness. I must apologise for my indifference lately. Most probably due to my indisposition I felt during waking hours. Had to open your Xmas card, not being able to wait, and it is very sweet. I will read and re-read it when I'm feeling low and lonely. We are always under much pressure. All love, N.

Air Mail   28 December 1944

Our second anniversary. Our Christmas finished well with a funny and good pantomime. We are not so hard pressed in work now – guess it's the slowing of operations due to bad weather here. In between my last letter to you I've had three air mails and an influx of other mail and cards. You will see and hear that we have moved the line on. We are still a fixture with plenty of work to do as usual and for some time to come. The weather remains poor. Many thanks for the books and paper. I've recently had a letter of 20 October, strange to say. A parcel from Aunt Emma had taken fifteen weeks. Recently we have had lectures by the MO on VD. As far as I know our company is clear. The penalty of any contraction means a program of two years before being allowed home, so that should be a deterrent. We get TT and TAB every year and a Typhus boost every six months and vaccinations every so often. We have moved on again. The countryside is simply wreckage. Loving you, N.

Air Mail   14 January 1945

Just had a good bath, or its equivalent, so feel fit and comfortable to write to you. Whilst I remember, could you possibly get me a comb, a jar of shaving cream and a fountain pen nib, please.

Thanks for your happy thoughts for me at the turn of the year. I'm afraid I was snoring my head off at the end of the old year, as the army generally does whenever possible. Your photo hasn't turned up yet, but guess it will any day now. Several of the boys have new photos of their wives and girls on show. Another of our chaps from Birmingham has had notification that his wife has a child three months old. My correspondence course papers have arrived so will now be busy swotting; hope I manage OK. I'd 200 cigarettes from *May* the other day.

161

Today I've heard from young Ken, Mr and Mrs A.'s son – he's in France. At last I've heard from my old boss, Frank H, so will have plenty to do in the pen line. Bye for now. All love, N.

May was evacuated from London with her two daughters to Norman's village, staying with Jack's mother. This was in the early part of the war. Jack was only five days or so out of his reservists time and in France when the Germans swept through it. Norman was very kind to May and the girls during this time. This little family were precious to us; we always spoke of Jack as Uncle.

Air Mail   18 January 1945

I'm speechless. I can't breath and my collar's tight and I can't do a thing about it. Yes, your photo has arrived and I'm unable to take my eyes off it. I was trying to forget the real you. I've locked you out of sight twice and had to dig you out again. You could never look more beautiful. I'd surely die without you.

My man went on in this strain and it was and is embarrasing to continue quoting his reaction. If it made him happy, he needed to be. How he ever managed to cope with the stresses and strains during this dreadful war is beyond me.

Air Mail   24 January 1945

Can't understand why my mail to you is taking so long. A lot of our lads are waiting. It may be due to the putrid flying weather. I get a rise in pay after three years in the army and can do with it, if it's only to swell the bank account. Nearly everyone has had leave in Rome at sometime, so guess it won't be long before it's my turn. Have read it somewhere that a Member of Parliament thinks and expects we are getting seven days' leave a year whilst serving!!

I feel sure that at some time I've told you about one of my pals marrying an Italian girl; if I'm repeating myself forgive. He lives in a village near Scunthorpe and was married on 6 January at Gualdo Todino. His wife, now an English subject, will be shipped to England. Funny do, hope they'll live happily when all's over. There's no sign of us moving and have been here ten weeks. All my love, N.

Air Mail   3 February 1945

Mail is coming through again after hanging fire and I've received yours of 20, 22 and 27 January. As I'm doing a twenty four hour guard on a stupid beggar who got drunk and did several other things, will try and answer yours. I'm amply rewarded if my letter of 18 January gave you much pleasure, so thank you for writing such a lovely letter in reply – this damnable parting. During my guard break I'm hoping to answer Mum for a parcel and two letters from relatives. By all accounts you've had a rough winter. We are in a sticky mess after a good deal of rain. Tatta and love, N.

Air Mail   8 February 1945

Last night I sent off a green letter containing some templates for a chair I've just made for the C in C. Quite plain in oak with bright upholstered back pad and removable seat. Please save them so that when in civvy street I can knock up one from it. Have had your letters of 29 and 31 January, also heard from Wing again. If you can manage to send a small bottle of sauce sometime please – a little something to put that extra taste in food.

Rocca Secca near Cassino is the place I returned to after my Yellow Period in hospital and the photo I've sent was taken at this place. Two of the lads have been 'mentioned in despatches' for work over a period. Both are sawyers; it's no mean job pushing heavy timber through big saws all day in the heat we have experienced out here. The correspondence course I'm doing is on measurement of builders' work specifications, contracts and quantities. All of which I may need when back home. An articled surveyor here says this is the best course. I'll be with you again soon. Love, N.

Air Mail   12 February 1945

Could you send me some fountain pen nibs or better still a pen. The old one had done good service and will no longer fill. It stalled as I was writing to Bobby Robson. Do please take care of yourself. You know you are only made like other people and can't go cracking on forever in all elements without a strain somewhere.

Yes, I named you to vote for me. We must all take this seriously if only to make a better go of it after the war. The *Picture Posts* haven't arrived. Mum sent a bundle of mails yesterday. As ever yours, N.

Air Mail   17 February 1945

Congratulations on the savings you have made. Seems ages since we started. The money paid into our business venture when I get my release and the building land paid is quite something, along with the bank account.

The fool we had in the clink has been more lucky than he deserved. we all expected him to get a stretch of detention; instead he has fourteen days' pay stopped.

I doubt if he will have learned his lesson. You have been to see Mr and Mrs A. Jack says he's about to plant border trees on the plot if he hasn't already done so, also the beech hedge. Bye and all love, N.

Air Mail 21 February 1945

Someone has written and said it is rumoured that I'll be coming home on leave soon – this is not so. I am at this time remembering two years ago almost when last I saw you. So I have memories of that time having walked twelve miles and still able to whistle and disturb your slumber.

We are still a fixture and up to our eyes in work. Had a football match against the South Africans on Sunday and won 5-2. Very enjoyable but it has stiffened me up. After a lovely sunny day tonight is frosty, so have to stoke up again. Waiting for your mail. All love, N.

Air Mail 26 February 1945

I have just served one year as a joiner. At long last my leave to Rome is here. My next letter will be from the Holy City. We leave tomorrow at 9.30 a.m. We will be in a truck for two hours, then leave this side for Rome at 1.00 p.m., travelling through the night, arriving at 7.00 a.m. the next day. We then leave on the following Wednesday, same times, same way, in all a break of ten days from work. I intend making the most of it. The opera, current shows, Vatican, St Peters, catacombs, forum, Colosseum, etc. A drink or two and lazy mornings in

165

bed. There are twenty six of us going, think it must be the last round up. Leave has started for Florence, but I've been hanging fire for Rome. All love, N.

I've neglected you dreadfully, so do please forgive, it's awkward to find moments of privacy and time when others are urging you to go off somewhere. I'm a little worried as I've grave doubts of you getting this for your birthday on the 12th. All the best in your ripe old age and do hope you get my present in time. You will see by my letter heading that I'm in Rome. City of What! Art, beauty and culture – that's the impression – and so it is but there's another side I prefer not to relate. I have seen a few English and Italian shows, walked miles. Been round the Vatican City and its store of treasures and inside many churches of note, seeing work of reputed masters and tomorrow visiting St Peter's. We return Wednesday. The train journey was rather awful, eighteen hours in the same compartment with half an hour's break for a meal on the way. I didn't manage a wink of sleep, we were so packed in. Actually it was all very good, I'm not complaining. We've had photos taken but they'll have to be sent on. The weather has been good and warm until today. A cold wind made us resort to overcoats which become heavy with walking. All love, N.

In normal times my man never suffered discomfort easily. The Italian train seating was bare wood. The others managed to sleep. Norman had threaded his long scarf through the luggage rack and was resting his head in the loop. When George who sat opposite woke up, he thought Norman had hung himself!

166

Air Mail   13 March 1945

Hope you received your flowers on your birthday. If not you'll think I've forgotten it again. Whilst on the subject of birthdays could you once again forward the date of Mum's. I'm ashamed to admit I've forgotten the day, but know it's in April. Bill Dove asked if I would mind you and he meeting if it could be arranged, as he would like to see you again. He is often in Leeds, Huddersfield, Sheffield, etc., so I've given him your address and here is his enclosed. I'd rather like to think of you both having a good chat about his wife and 'our John' and me. He's a private with a number back in the homeland, lucky beggar. I'm sending off some photos of the Rome trip by ordinary mail. The C in C, dear, is the Commander-in-Chief, the top-of-the-tops, Field Marshall Alexander. All love, N.

By a separate leter of this date, the 13th, this is a covering note for the enclosed photos taken in Rome. So I'll add the necessary information.

No. 1 exhibit is a programme of a show we saw.

No. 2 a sketch of a soldier for which I paid 5s. (25p) when slightly oiled. Might be me, but then might be anybody, but I assure you I was able to sit quite still.

No. 3 is of three of us, me on the end with the tash, the middle fellow my mate, the other one of our boys from Wigan, whose greatest wish is for a fish and chip supper! He also says he will raise his cap to Wigan Gas Works each time he sees it after this.

No. 4. A masterpiece this, every inch a soldier even when blinded by the sunlight. You will note the new fashion in ties, the medal ribbon; he was in Africa you know. You will note the sunken cheeks from army feeding and the tendency to baldness which I've repeatedly warned you of. He sends his best love to you.

No. 5 was taken in the grounds of the Vatican City with St Peter's in the background. It is of a whole party of which only five are us, as it were. Looking at the photo I'm second from the right, front row. Johnny Lockhart is the one with the baldy head next to me, a grand little Scotch laddie. Directly behind him is the Wigan boy. Next to him with hands folded in front is our goal keeper, Len Harvey, from Stoke. Three along from him smiling broadly is my living, working and sleeping mate, George Harvison from Louth.

No.6 and last is another party taken this time in front of one of the Triumphant Arches, erected the Lord knows how long ago, said to be in Caesar's reign. In the background, behind the RAF officer, is the forum. On the right in the corner, if one can have a corner of a round building, is the Colosseum, equally as old and historical. Just off the photo is the Appian Way. To the right one would see one of the hills on which Rome is situated. So this is rather an historical and famous spot upon which we are standing. That's all, dear. Love, N.

My man hadn't changed one bit, his baldness etc., a mere joke and the pleasure was mine to see him looking happy. My post lady used at times to put on Norman's incoming letters, 'Not known at this address', or 'Never heard of her.' She was a sweetie and I was soon to miss her.

.

Air Mail   21 March 1945

The mimosa trees were in full bloom in Rome. After being here four months we moved a little nearer home and you. It is quite a lovely place, but rather noisy. Nearly all grass. Once again under canvas. Makes a difference and the fact it is perfect weather, really warm and stripped to the waist. Thanks for the parcel – all seems intact, but the comb broken in two.

Haven't really sorted the contents out yet. Have managed a present from Rome for you. Things were paltry for the price but you will find two cameo rings, a brooch for you and Mum and Mrs A. which you can take when visiting and the photos to show them. I'll send them when I get the chance as we are busy getting things in order here. Uncle George has died in great pain, I'm told, and there's a whisper he may have left me his tools. He had promised to have a pint with me when I got back. As always, N.

Air Mail   25 March 1945

Have heard from you at last. Today I've sent off the little parcel – it could take three weeks. The things looked cheaper each time I looked at them. The rings were 1400 lira or £3 10s. 0d. (£3.50). I was assured they were real silver and cameo. I have my doubts but unable to afford anything more costly. There's a lot of fiddling goes on here when buying things. I've had a couple of hours off this afternoon and beat another of our sections at football 4-1. Boastful fellow. I captained the winning team, eh what! All love, N.

Air Mail   29 March 1945

Fancy! A letter of the 23rd has arrived from you and you haven't heard from me, but I bet you did next day. That's how it happens with me. Thanks for Mum's birth date. I had to ask you in haste last year. A diary is what I need if you can get one; I need to record addresses too.

We had smashing weather up to a few days ago. Now it is dull and bags of rain, including an all night session of it and woke to half flooded landscape. But glory be, our tents are up on a hill and we were very snug. In any case the sun has shone all day and shows promises of better weather. The green parts are pushing up and a mass of fruit trees in blossom, almond I imagine. A pair of pea fowl, a cock and hen, at a nearby farm are making the most continuous screeching noise – never heard anything like it. Quite out of keeping with the beautiful plumage of the cock's tailspread of about four feet. Mum and Aunt Loui are seeing some relatives at Driffield and I believe are living like fighting cocks. Seems no rationing deep in the country. All love, N.

Air Mail   2 April 1945

It's Easter Monday and a beautiful evening and has been the last three days. We finished dinner time yesterday and played against another company, winning 4-1. Today we finished at 4.30 p.m. and watched our officers and senior NCOs who played HQ officers and NCOs. Very funny indeed. I doubt if any of the twenty two had ever played before. Myself and another laddie were in attendance with Red Cross jeep and flag, axe and cross-cut saw, a huge bell and gallons of water. We had plenty of emergencies. If you read the papers lately you will know where I am. There's no sign of leave yet, so don't bank on it coming off. All love, N.

Air Mail   6 April 1945

Our post is smashing just now, I'd your so lovely letter of the 2nd today, posted on the 3rd. I believe our air mail goes without stamp up to one ounce in weight. Over an ounce it costs about sixpence ($2\frac{1}{2}$p). At any rate it is all by air, as is your incoming mail. You should be paying $1\frac{1}{2}$d. ($\frac{1}{2}$p), but enquire at your post office. An ordinary from Bill Dove dated as yours arrived by the same post. I've just had to knock off a bit whilst things quietened down, but all's well – a miss is as good as a mile. We are still getting a chance to play football. The other night a laddie broke his right tibia in the fray. It was very much deformed and my first aid came in useful. As always, N.

Air Mail   11 April 1945

I've your letters of the 6th and 8th to answer. We have met our doom, having won so many matches. Knew it would happen shortly. Playing Fienza Town in the stadium, lost 5-3. They were a better team, I cannot say otherwise. Italian professionals spend all their time training. Two of them came from Milan University. We didn't expect meeting crack professionals. For various reasons we had two substitutes and a goalie. We were rather awed by the magnitude of the stadium and about 3000 spectators. If we haven't moved on, we expect to meet them again in a week. You will know we have started up again out here. Once more I haven't answered your letters but think you would rather know what's happening to me and I've noted what you have said especially. With dearest love, N.

Air Mail   19 April 1945

Glad the parcel arrived and it was intact. I cannot get it out of my head how cheap the things looked. Glad Betty liked the powder, I suppose she could have got it anywhere. Yes, we made a good joke about the officers and NCOs' match, it was marvellous. We had another similar last night. Two teams of men who had never played before. It was a perfect scream; half of them are cripples today. One funny instance was when the goalkeeper, six foot and round-shouldered, with a terrific hooked nose and buck teeth, stopped the ball, fell into the upright and the bar dropped down, crowning him,

171

and someone dashed up and scored! Pardon my ignorance in relating this but it was terribly funny to watch. It is teriffically hot now and we are in training for the big match on Sunday with the Italian pros who gave us our first defeat in over two years. I've just had a shower – rather Heath Robinson but smashing. Our nights are quieter with the front moving, but I expect we will be off again one fine day. I've heard from your Mum and Dad, please thank them for me. As always, N.

Air Mail   22 April 1945

Glad the trees are in and glad you recompensed JA. Check on the beech cuttings that Dad and I put in. Presuming you have taken a photo of the plot and will send me and refresh my memory of that delightful spot. Thank you for all you have done for my mother personally. I'll try and give her a hint on only doing what is necessary, but doubt if it will do any good. It's unfair she knock herself up and then expect you to help her out. Bye for now, N.

Air Mail   25 April 1945

We have just won the knock-out competition – at football, of course – beating the Palestinians 3-0. I'll be sending on some more photos of the Fienza Town match. The return match I was all talk of didn't come off. The army has moved up and that Italian stadium is being used for some other purpose and civilians are not allowed near.

Your last two letters remain unanswered, rambling off as I do, please accept my apology. The correspondence course is at a standstill as I was browned off with each course number not being consistent. I'd written and pointed out this was happening. I have heard good reports of my mate's Italian

172

wife by those who have seen her. She is, of course, still here in Italy. It's colossal what you unearthed from that old settee, dear.

Keep happy dear. It might not be much longer. N.

It certainly was an old settee. The springs had gone and to make it as comfortable as possible there were 2 slips of carpet, 1 dressing gown, 4 cardigans, 3 skirts and 8 pairs of holey socks inside it! C.

Air Mail   8 May 1945

It's Victory Day I do believe at last! I'm sorry to say I don't feel a bit excited. There isn't anything to celebrate with, so all we can do is have the day off. In civilian life, no doubt, I'd be patting everyone on the back and having a drink. On Thursday, Friday and Saturday we decorated a local hall and on Sunday we had a dance in it from 8 till 12. It was quite a good do. I was merely an onlooker. Preceeding the dance in the afternoon we had another football match against the Italians, winning 9-3. On Monday morning we were up by 4.00 a.m., eight of us, and off to Venice, arriving by 9.00 a.m., spending the day there and were back by 9.00 p.m. I truly say it ws a most enjoyable day. In fact the most enjoyable day I've had in the army. Venice is marvellous, I haven't the space to describe it all. We went by gondola up the Grand Canal where the battles of flowers takes place. Went round San Marco, a wonderful cathedral and the Doge's Palace, across the Bridge of Sighs and saw lots of interesting things. The shops hadn't any shortages, wines were plentiful. I managed what I thought were two decent things and will send them off as soon as possible, along with your ring from Florence. The first is a necklace for Mum which I know you will forward. The second a bracelet which I had to have – it also cleaned me out. I'm told it is gold and silver filigree and every bit handworked. I've only room to say that your last letter had the snaps in and I think very good. I went to bed with miserable thoughts of our prolonged parting – and the war being over, I wanted to rejoice with you alone. I expect we shall soon be moving North again from this big valley. Bye love, N.

Air Mail   9 May 1945

It's a few days ago since we moved from Florence. It's been dull and raining and we had two hours of continuous snow on the mountains. It was when we dropped down into the valley that we found the war was over with Germany. There was much rejoicing amongst the locals. We made camp after being on the road nine hours. My mate had my bivouac ready and I got my bed down and plopped into it. We are wondering what will happen here. Will we get leave and then go out East. We are carrying on the same; in fact if it wasn't for the Italians we wouldn't believe it was over. However, it will be pleasing for you to know another campaign is over. Keep happy and all love, N.

Ordinary Letter   10 My 1945

I've never had such pleasure in sending you a parcel since being at Bari. With the end of the fight things are much easier and we are having a bit of time off – today in full. The last lot have gone off to Venice. We're all packed up for a move which we believe is back down Italy. This isn't very pleasing to us, but we aren't grumbling at all at present. We are continuing being occupational troops whilst at the same time the demobilisation of low units will start and we hope keep going on. With us having had nearly two and a half years overseas, only the lads joining us all the time will be required for the Far East after a month's home leave. Low group men will be sent for release and middle, like myself will, I think and hope, not have to go East or continue as garrison troops until release group turn comes. That is the situation as I know it, dear, and I'll keep you posted of all and any further information. I doubt I'll see you before next year; don't let this upset you. The snaps you sent are so good and your mum looks nice. You could hardly think she could 'knock my face off', bless her. I was happy to show my pals the lovely views and trees of home. I'm not unduly elated by the extra stripe, but it means I get extra cash and a few privileges. I haven't had it long and think I'll not retain it long. My mates are asking if you have now moved into a larger house! Thanks for the promised parcel. I'll drink your health when the lemon crystals arrive. It is boiling hot and I'm like a lobster. Hope you have a good holiday, you deserve it. Twelve pages, we are told, weigh about an ounce for air mail, and as I'm on the thirteenth I'd better finish. That's all dear, keep cheery. Love, N.

Air Mail   14 May 1945

I do hope my mail is reaching you. My incoming mail isn't too good, though I'm not alarmed. With such momentous happenings, troop movements and the feeding of the populace, etc., it is to be expected. I don't think I've had such a long wait for your letters. Yesterday was a day off and a truck load of us went back to Bologna, which is rather badly battered. I couldn't find anything worth buying for you and spent a good bit of time in a NAAFI, which was OK. In the afternoon I saw an Ann Sheridan film, *Shine on Harvest Moon*, which was quite good. Since getting back have had a meal, then made myself comfortable with a shave and wash-down in cold water – delicious and appreciated after the heat of the day, which is terrific. I'm doing as in Africa, sleeping in the nude and pulling up a blanket when I wake cold in the morning.

175

I've heard that the first group is being released on the 21st of this month. I'd said we were expecting to move in my last letter. This is not so and we are still a fixture and seem likely to be. That's all dear. Not very interesting I'm afraid. All love, N.

Green Letter   16 May 1945

We have been working hard and long and so have today off. I was spending it in bed until nature forced me up at midday and found myself bathed in perspiration. I'd had breakfast in bed, brought by one of the cooks who was with me at Elgin. After retiring again after lunch and dozing away, your mail arrived with photo enclosed. That did upset the apple cart. I'll try to answer your two previous letters, which I've failed to answer, mainly through stress of work. You will now know that I'm at the top of my trade in the army – so I've made it after all. It has been embarrassing to receive compliments from the OC personally. I know when I've done a good job. On the strength of my increased 'salary', I intend keeping it for you in case I should ever get back to Rome, which I think is quite possible. You might find out how much I have in this world and let me know as I'd hate to have to ask you for the means of a pint. Very happy that you think of me so often. It's a damned good job you aren't being tossed about in a truck or sleeping under a bivouac. We have flies, numerous species of spider, ants by the million, mosquitos, daddy long legs, midges and hundreds of lizards in lovely colours sliding all over the place. There's a few snakes said not to be poisonous. I killed a black scorpion although it wasn't near my tent; awful things, make you cringe. No, I don't smoke much, though I get allocations from the army and NAAFI. I've had 600 pinched and still have left over a thousand. Whilst watching a good football team the other night against an inferior, we were given a perfect display by a left winger,

176

scoring four goals himself. It turned out to be Pattison of Queens Park and Motherwell. It is time to put nets down and insect repellant on all exposed skin and I've no wish to get malaria. I love you and always will, N.

Air Mail   18 May 1945

It seems at least a fortnight since I heard from you and Mum, and then last night I heard from you both. It seems my mail isn't getting through to you very well. You have bluebells out again; they bring back memories too and you had the pitcher full of them in your bedroom for your weekend from Lincoln. I think of cherry and almond blossoms. Here we have the almonds and they are already quite big and also cherries which look and taste glorious. I raid them most days of the week – do wish you could see them. Such colour. The most remarkable thing is that the birds never seem to raid them and we have nightingales, tits and sparrows. I don't know how to account for this.

I cannot see me being out of the army for at least another year, so don't get upset – I am stating facts. All love, N.

PS I'm about to go to a rest camp at Lake Garda for four days, it's near the Brenner Pass. I'll be coming back as you go to Blackpool for your break. N.

I took Norman's mother and mine off to Blackpool for the change. We had a pleasant time. His mother took her knitting on the sands and lost a needle. Next morning she insisted that when the tide was out she would find it, which she did to our surprise! Quite unbelievable. Others on this part of the beach saw the amazing find and began searching for bits and pieces! Quite, quite funny.

Green Letter 15 June 1945

I'd just written my last letter to you when your parcel arrived intact. Well, we left camp on Wednesday morning about 8.00 a.m., arriving here about dinner time. 'Here' is a villa tight on the lakeside with a little jetty running out and on which we have fixed a diving board and ladder. On the lake there are two rubber dinghies, two German storm boats with outboard motors, one English assault boat with German engine and lastly a beautiful job that doesn't half move and which we converted ourselves and painted in two lovely shades of blue. The food is smashing, no more than usual, but we supplement it with eggs, of which I've had seven today. The lake is reputed to be about 1000 metres deep and slopes rapidly in the first ten feet or so. When I dive I've got to swim but I don't risk it far. The water is beautifully clear and chocker with fish of all sizes. The water is as cold as can be expected because of its depth.

A letter from Bill Dove said he had heard from you. One from Mother, who sounds all worked up about her holiday with you. This letter, along with my last, will be awaiting you on your return and hoping you've had a smashing time. We are feeling somewhat ruffled at the treatment dished out to us at our last billets. Twenty five of us, seven NCOs and eighteen men refused point-blank to go into the present billets against sergeants' and sergeant majors' orders to move in. It was touch and go whether we would be put under close arrest and court-martialled, but we conceded to the OC, who in all fairness could have had us all in. The fly in the ointment at present is a company of military police, three weeks out from England, trying to do their best to make us into home station troops by all kinds of petty charges, i.e., not having sleeves rolled down after 7.30 p.m., shirt neck unbuttoned, being out a few minutes after curfew and the Lord knows damned what. I'll be glad to call my soul my own one day.

I am sending you some snaps of the Lake. Did try and get you a present but failed. There are only villages in this area with nothing much but wine and eggs, ice cream and a barber's shop. Perhaps I didn't tell you that I'd heard from Tom Altoft who is in 5 Corps in Austria now and was in North Africa and the Eighth Army when we were and also in the old First Army and I never knew it. This is the end of my pad so have to sign off with my love to you, as always. N.

Air Mail   17 June 1945

Have had your letters of 28, 29 May, 2 June, so thanks a lot. Just the stuff to give a weary soldier. I've heard from Bert W who tells me that all but one of our village prisoners have arrived home, except one who has arrived in England. It will give much happiness and rejoicing in a few homes. A letter from Wink O after all these months. Our letters will have crossed. I'm not to write to him again at Naples. His dad is to try to get Wink's release to help in the business. Old Bruce is somewhere in the wilds and I've managed a line or two off to him. I'm hoping the service can trace him. In my next letter I hope to tell you about this place. As always, N.

Ordinary Letter   21 June 1945

In my last letter I said I would tell you about this place. It is quite a new sanatorium in its own beautiful grounds and has been used, I believe, exclusively for the treatment of rheumatism. There are hot sulphur springs in the grounds, a series of outdoor baths, some mud baths at different temperatures, all about four foot six inches deep and apparatus to submerge patients. We have two of the coolest baths to use for swimming and have half an hour at midday and before dinner at night and later when we can swim again or play cricket. The wards have beds of six with two hand basins with hot and cold water. Each floor has its toilets, duty room, etc. The walls are tiled and there are terrazzo floors. We have a metal locker, a chair, a bed with mattress and pillow. On the ground floor are foot treatment baths. The kitchens are in the basement and are very modern. There's an operating theatre and morgue and laundry nearby and a very imposing chapel. Every room in this building has a crucifix. The place is run by white-clothed Sisters of Mercy, I suppose, but why they trollope about in all those clothes I don't know, it must be very unhygenic. In some of the lakes and pools in the grounds there are frogs and fish. Trees surround the area, a general variety like ours. By far the most glorious are the magnolias, now in full bloom. The flowers have a beautiful coloured stamen in the centre of these lovely white petals. A truly marvellous sight. A thing of note also is the Turkish bath, hewn out of solid rock. Boiling water rushes up from what seems like volcanic elements and it is almost impossible to breathe amongst it. All this being put to the use of curing mankind. We thought we were entitled after years of campaigning and prepared to spend some time here, but our friends in authority decreed otherwise and now after a week of it have had to get out within forty eight hours, so that our German prisoners can use the place, and we will go back to the boiling sun, flies and tents. I'll say no more, but remain yours, N.

Air Mail   23 June 1945

Our weather is absolutely boiling and at night I'm sleeping naked under the nets. Hope you have had good weather and holiday. Nothing much fresh to report here. I saw *For Whom the Bell Tolls* the other night at Padua, with Gary Cooper and Ingrid Bergman – she was glorious. Padua is a large town, street cars are running, all lights on, bags of shops and stalls. Saw the first batch of tomatoes on sale at 60 lira, about 1s. 6d. a pound, ($7\frac{1}{2}$p).

I'm still trying to find silk stockings. I've been out to the River Po today surveying, and again tomorrow bridging. Will be with you soon. Love N.

Air Mail   27 June 1945

Excuse pencil. I'm at Lake Garda again, but working with a lance corporal electrician to do alteration lighting and another laddie covering in the flat roof of the dining room against the sun. We expect to be here a couple of days. This letter has to go back with the leave party to the company. I'd no idea I was coming here until shortly before setting off. One of your letters of 12th May had gone astray and arrived after 17 June. I found your boating antics very funny whilst you were on holiday with Mum, having to take over in mid-stream.

Will be with you again soon. N.

Norman's mum used to row at Hempholme where her dad was lock-keeper and the family lived. We had hired a boat, the three of us and two other ladies wished to join. Me, supposed to be capable of rowing, and four terror-stricken folk, who shifted about in the boat forever trying to get comfortable and changing seats as I tried to row. I almost tipped the boat over at a tricky turn, so Mother-in-Law took over and I didn't think I was such a clever girl after all! A watcher in a motor-boat kept a little distance away.

Air Mail   7 July 1945

I have been able to record my own vote for the British government. Our ASM, CQMS and a sergeant left for demobbing and home this morning. Lucky blighters, but all

181

are over forty and have been in since 1939. Their groups are 8 and 9. All up to the 16s group have had their demob medicals. It's a hell of a long way off for the 37s. Still in the same place. We have now constructed a limited size bathing pool. I was working all weekend on a rush job, but expect time off later. It's Friday the 13th, but I'll risk it. It is so hot, so very hot, and concentration in writing is difficult. The River Po is almost dried up. Forgot to mention that Padua sports ATS girls. I noted when last in town. Be tolerant with me in my frustrations. Keep the mail coming. As far as I know the air graph service is being discontinued. Air mail service includes anything under 12ozs incoming and outgoing.

29 July 1945

I hear today that the Eighth Army ceases to exist, so presumably we are just occupation troops. The leave in the United Kingdom that you speak of is quite true and has been operating for sometime. Twenty eight days at home, journey via land each way to Calais and Folkestone. If under 21 group, not eligible on account of nearness to demob. When it gets to my turn so many will be picked out of the hat. In the meantime anything can happen. We are still busy and no rumours of movement. Bye dearest, Love, N.

Air Mail   2 August 1945

August again and into the kind of weather we both enjoy. Wouldn't it be grand if I did get leave this autumn. My favourite song at the moment is, 'There's no Place Like Home'. My early years was 'The Desert Song'. The heat and the desert has left me with rather a croak and difficulty in singing 'One Alone' or 'Lover Come Back to Me.' Previous to this last week I've been passionately fond of tomatoes. Here they are making and tinning soup literally in tons. I've scoffed my share whilst here. Now I hate the smell and sight of them and think I'll never eat another. That's all dear. Who knows and keep up with the exercises. Always yours, N.

6 and 7 August 1945

It's just started raining and even if it keeps it up for a week I doubt if it will make any difference or impression. Everything is so cracked, hard and dry. It will freshen things up if nothing else, especially for tonight when we have a corps match. I am including the photos when we played Fienza Town. I've a bit of tea to get and we leave for Rovigo at 5.30 p.m., returning after 9.00 p.m.

It's now Bank Holiday Monday and what a day. Work as usual and still raining. I'd hoped to get an ordinary off to enable me to answer yours. Think it will have to wait for an opportunity. I'm sorry if I've cribbed about your letters, it's such a grand thrill to receive them and so miserable if none arrive. No, dear, I didn't see our King in the parade. All traffic was off the road for him to pass and I'm told it took hours to sort out. Not much to tell you about myself, so please don't worry. Be with you one day. Love, N.

Air Mail   14 August 1945

I've some requests to make. Will you get me a fountain pen please and the following: *Your MP* by Gracchus, *Now Pray We For Our Country* by Eric Knight and *Rosie Todmarsh* by Adrian Alington. Having read all three, I'd like them for the future. My mum might like to read *Rosie Todmarsh*. Glad you are getting plenty of fresh air and exercise. I'm placing so much on my English womanhood – can't stand the blokes

183

who compare the local girls here. We won against a Cheshire team last night, 4-1. Another match tomorrow night, but we don't expect to win as a few of our team are on leave at different places. Love, N.

Air Mail   26 August 1945

I'm going on a second week to Lake Garda tomorrow, so my next letter will be from there and expect a lazy week. Wishing you were with me. We did have a couple of days off to celebrate VJ day, so spent most of it in bed. One night went to a show which was not good. We are still sending men home in driblets of twos and threes. Our NAAFI is up today and I'm about to enjoy a whole bottle of beer. Love, N.

Air Mail   3 September 1945

It's a queer life this, being in the army. Last time I wrote to you I was about to go to Lake Garda for a week. I'd only been there half the time when I had to return to the company and come right up here to Udine on a three weeks' course of PT, sports, and organising. As you will see my letterhead says 'PT and Sports Centre' CMF. It's rather hectic at times, but very interesting, for we have to learn from scratch. It includes swimming, wrestling, rugby, soccer, softball, basketball, track events and sports meetings. There are bags of lectures. So roughly speaking we spend half our time stripped in shorts, chasing about, and the other attending lectures on everything. We are a mixed set up. I'm the only RE, but there are officers, WOs, sergeants, Americans, South Africans and junior NCOs from all mobs in the old Eighth army and we look a very mixed bag with so many different Cap Badges and Shoulder Flashes. A rather funny incident happened yesterday. I'd paired up with a tall laddie from the Sixth Armoured Division and went and saw *The Constant Nymph* and then on to supper. He was from Hull and knows quite a few of the lads I do footballing. He worked at Blackburns and knows a lot of our village blokes, including the old Duke, where he spent a while on his leave. Do excuse all this about myself, dear. No mail from you to answer, but expect it being forwarded. Bye love, N.

Air Mail   7 September 1945

What a life as a junior NCO – I've to do guard here as we are the lowest rank with there being no privates or the like. This course has turned out to be quite decent, though rather hectic. There are nine periods, five in the morning and four in the afternoon. Reveille is at 6.30 a.m. and we return for a meal at 5.00 p.m. No letters from you but that's due to my movements. Keep on writing to normal address. Heats are taking place today (Saturday) and I am writing this through the dark hours. The finals are on Sunday. A letter from Mum says she hopes you will go over. Our pear and apple trees are bearing ready-to-eat fruit. I'm lagging behind with my notes. I'm afraid the two picture houses here are very tempting. I've seen *Rebecca*, which was very enjoyable. Keep smiling. Love, N.

Letter   15 September 1945

I have had your letters of the 2nd and 5th so now more up to date. I'm still in Udine. A letter from your Mum and Dad has arrived, which I will answer in due course. Please will you thank them for me. Good for you getting the fruit bottled. Hope I'm home to sample some soon. Pleased you have received the two sets of table mats. I'd almost forgotten about them, seems ages since I sent them off. It was a joint affair – a Manchester laddie painted the designs and I finished with the polishing. We like to do a bit of something for the future. The material is Masonite but will burn under pressure. I plan our kitchen design sometimes – always with our future in mind. I get awfully frustrated and it must most certainly be apparent to you. We have this weekend off and Monday start our last week here. It is still rather rough going. A sports meeting this Sunday between the Navy, RAF, Army and New Zealand Forces, so hope to see some good running. See you one day soon. All love, N.

Letter   19 September 1945

We've had glorious weather for at least a week and it's time I wrote to you again. I don't advocate you making Mum an allowance; in fact I don't believe it necessary. Yet I'm pleased you give her cash to show your independence when over visiting her. As far as I know she has sufficient and would have told me otherwise if she felt that way. I'm sending two more paper money samples. The browny-red is Austrian and worth 3d. (1p), and the grey-green is German, valued at 6d ($2\frac{1}{2}$p), but we are not using them. In Italy it's still the old lira. Bye my love, N.

Letter   23 September 1945

Your letters of the 13th and 17th were waiting my return and I have further news. We finished the course on Friday night. My truck arrived Saturday lunchtime and the driver said how the company felt a move was in the offing. We arrived back in time for the evening meal and lo and behold he was right. It's not a bad as it sounds, but we are off to Greece. Last night we saw another lot go on leave and today we have been packing up. We set off in the morning on a three day run to Bari-Bari of all places, our first real port of call in Italy and it's two years to the day since we landed in Italy. It's from Bari that we sail for Greece. The course I've just finished is simply to teach junior NCOs like me to teach respective units in games and PT when physical activity is low and to keep the troops fit. I find this kind of exercise enjoyable. I'll try and keep you posted and as always all my love, N.

Air Mail   27 September 1945

What a life! Things have been in such a rush I hardly know where I am. On the way to Bari we had lunch at Ancona and stayed the night in Catholica. Do you remember us staying here before or wasn't I able to tell you in those days? Next morning after being on guard all night, we were off again. It wasn't a very good day with cold winds and very cloudy. We reached Ortona and stayed the night. Away again Wednesday morning, had lunch at Termoli. This was one of our old haunts. Finishing twenty miles south of Foggia in rain and bitterly cold winds. This morning we started off a little later as our destination was only sixty miles away. But Oh Lord, how it rained! We were here for lunch. The trucks are in a vehicle park and we in a transit camp and have had lunch, a bath, shaved and cleaned up. I'm saving my clean clothes for the end of the journey. I don't know how long we will be here, possibly hours or days 'till the boat is ready. Then off to Greece. I can't say I'm looking forward to it. No change of address, so write as usual and don't worry. Love, N.

Air Mail   1 October 1945

The transport is all on board and the half of us go on tomorrow. A cargo boat takes two to two and a half days, a troopship about thirty six hours, I'm told, but still will not know when we sail. Rumour says we are going just outside

Athens. Rumour also says we are off to build bridges, fell timber and build winter quarters for occupational troops. The OC is on leave with several others. 18 group left yesterday. I'm looking forward to a bundle of letters at the other end. Money and language will be different in Greece. Bye love, N.

Air Mail   **Greece**   5 October 1945

We have arrived. Our address the same as before. Whilst at Bari saw the film, *Keys of the Kingdom* with Gregory Peck (a new name to me). We sailed on Tuesday about 7.30 p.m. A storm which had been blowing for forty eight hours had died away so we were lucky to have made a good crossing on Wednesday with nothing to report except for the many islands we passed on the way. Thursday we docked about 4.00 p.m. and had a short journey by train to this transit camp. I suppose when the other half arrive (they were still loading at Bari) the works will start and the sooner the better. The food is only just edible. We're sleeping rough and there's petty thieving and the loss of privacy such as you cannot imagine. We had landed at Piraeus, the port of Athens. Oh dear, it did look in a mess with poverty and the aftermath of war. The camp is on the outskirts and we haven't been allowed out yet. I'm told that Athens is very nice and lacks nothing. Being out of touch with no mail from you, I'm hoping you are fit and well. Love, N.

Air Mail   9 October 1945

Writing in pencil I've neither ink nor light and no mail yet. Parcels and papers are arriving. Our group 19's leave on the 12th for homeward journey and release. Tomorrow we should be moving into our new camp which we have been busy preparing this last three days. We have been issued with another blanket, so that's three in all. We will be under canvas on the edge of the sea so it seems it's going to be cold. We are to have lights installed and will be able to make ourselves more comfortable. The rest of the company arrived by air at their third attempt; the previous two had been turned back by bad weather conditions over the mountains. Our new camp is about half an hour's truck ride from the centre of Athens, where we have a good NAAFI, YMCA, and Garrison Theatre showing English and American Films with subtitles. Athens has plenty to drink and eat. A cabaret and shops full of all kinds of stuff. Longing for your letters. N.

Air Mail   13 October 1945

Good egg! I've a letter from you at last and one two days ago and also one from Mum yesterday. I'm writing whilst on guard. We are now established in our camp and things are getting quite shipshape. Quite a bit of work in.

I finished at 3.00 p.m. and managed my first swim. Tomorrow we are having the whole day off; if it's as grand as the last two days I'll be in the water again. The sea is still quite warm and very shallow for far enough without being out of depth. It is very salty and so exceedingly buoyant. So far I find the Greek goddesses few and far between. I have yet to see a smasher. Well, the language – here's the alphabet, twenty four words in rotation.

Although a lot of our letters are used they don't sound the same and are not pronounced the same. B is spelt Beta but pronounced *Vita*. I'll be worse with this than Italian. I'm enclosing 1 drachma, the smallest denomination and there are 100 of these for 1s. (5p). By the way, will you get me a diary, dear. Yes, Mrs A is a treasure, she never falters and is a great friend. We both appreciate we must show her we care. Yours as ever, N.

Air Mail   17 October 1945

Many thanks for your letters which are arriving OK, with the
exception of a fortnight's which seem to have gone for ever.
But it is possible for them to turn up, it's happened before.
Yes, my mum seemed to have looked on the black side at my
move but thanks to your assurance seems to be a bit better.
Leave has been cancelled for the time being as so many are
away. Sorry you cannot get the books I wrote about as you
say we may in the future. I am saving hard so that I shall
have a bob or two when I get home. That you are attending
to the many jobs I ask of you, thanks. All love, N.

Letter   21 October 1945

Sunday night and after a lovely day which we have spent
playing cricket. Yesterday we finished work at midday and
what I should think was all my back mail arrived, amongst
which were three from Mum and four from you. Some
correspondence papers returned, all of which I have to digest,
then lazed the afternoon away until time to wash, shave and
then tea-time. I saw *Union Pacific* in Athens. It was quite
good, then had a bottle of champagne, supper and wander
round and back to bed. Managed some more swimming in
transparent sea water. One can see the grains of sand on the
sea bottom. A few fish about and some jelly fish, but no one
has been stung.

We cooked fried onions and pilchards for tea with bread
and margarine. Now most of the men are in town I'm writing
to you. You're my sheet anchor when all seems lost. I've
always you there to comfort me, to help keep me straight all
these hundreds of miles away, when others fall by the wayside.
I always think and rely on you. You make me confoundedly
happy and knowing all your capabilities too. Glad to know
your rations are going up. Ours are coming down from

1 November. I'll let you know the result. Mum said how you both had enjoyed the trip to Hull Fair. Enclosed are few leaves of the eucalyptus tree. We rub them and smell them and it's quite refreshing. Leave is still at a standstill; more are expected back soon. I hope I can get home for Xmas and our anniversary. I have been down in the mouth about leave, so any grumpiness in my letters I hope you will overlook. All love, N.

25 and 29 October 1945

Always yearning for your letters. I've received one today of the 23rd and had one yesterday as well. Also one from your mum and dad. We have had the weekend off again. I went into Athens on Saturday evening and saw *Rulers of the Sea* which was about the introduction of steam instead of sail and then had the usual drink and supper.

Sunday morning I lazed, then played the Rest Camp at soccer, winning 5-1, dashing afterwards into this glorious sea prior to tea, then into Athens. The place was packed solid with Greeks celebrating 28 October on which day in 1940 they were asked to surrender by the Italians, but refused and fought on until they had just about trounced them when Hitler sent his forces and were at last overrun. So now 28 October is an annual affair. Athens was lit up brilliantly, flood lights on Parliament building, Royal Palace with soldiers in national costume, university, bank, Acropolis. It was almost impossible to move in Constitution Square, University and Churchill Street. I'm afraid I over-drank. All love, N.

Letter   2 November 1945

It's a funny old mail service. I'm without news of you and can't understand it as we are right on top of the aerodrome

– the only one in Greece. Planes are arriving and departing all and every day. On guard again last night. 'Crash H' is leaving tomorrow. He sent his wife to England when we left Italy and has now gone on compassionate leave because of his mother's illness. His wife is also pregnant. I have given him your address as he would like to see you. Crash used to travel miles on his motor bike to see his girl. I only saw her once. She adored him as he did her. Never have I seen such love light in anyone's eye as hers for Crash.

I have packed up a box of sultanas for you, Mum and Mrs A. Thought they would be useful for Xmas. All love, N.

Letter   6 November 1945

It has happened again after moaning and mail has arrived. I'm a new man! Today I'm feeling better after a rough couple of days. Typical army – there's a sudden decision for inoculations. I was one that required the lot. There are vaccinations later in the week. The enclosed snap is of a Wigan lad, Steve T, a Greek boy who helps us, Humphries, now on leave, and R. Lewis from Manchester, who has been on leave and T. Whalley, another lad from Manchester. Behind them is part of the workshop tent and part of an electric welding truck. I am more than pleased and relieved to have had such a nice letter from you. The fact that you are putting extra electricity points in Mum's house will help her. It's an all round approval.

On completion of my service for Class A release there's fifty six days leave plus a day for every month abroad. So if I reckon three years I shall have seventeen weeks in addition. Each day means full pay and allowances for wife and rations. This is something the home stationed chap doesn't get. If promotion comes, and it's wishful thinking, any rank held for a required period gets extra pay for all service allowance, etc.

Class B. I could ask for release to go back to my old job with my old boss applying for me at an earlier date than demob. Nobody is going to point a finger at me for finding an easy way out of the army. My late boss had asked me one day if I wanted still to be in a reserved occupation. I'd no idea I was – that's the truth – and said I didn't think it mattered, so was called up. That's all dear. The weather is very windy and much cooler now, though we are sweating midday, being further south, and two hours ahead of your time. As always yours, N.

Air Mail   10 November 1945

Your mail of 2 November arrived today and I have been waiting response to two of my previous letters to you. In this you acknowledge and make casual reference to them. No don't send any more parcels, it isn't really necessary. I'm sure to be home before long now. With regard to the all important question of leave, I've been chasing everyone so that I can calculate and hoping against hope that I'll be home before Xmas. There's lots of lads after me to go. Would you believe it, we had three reinforcements straight from England yesterday, having only been in the army a short while. I'm sorry if I seem a wet rag but I don't want to see any more faces other than friends and to spend all my time with you. I've had my fill of places and faces and I must get up to the plot and plan and square it up. All for now dear, N.

Letter   14 November 1945

What weather! I've no need to tell you after what you are having. Ours has been deadly with continual rain for two days and what rain! Lightning that runs all over the place and terrific thunder. Luckily our tent has kept fairly dry and have been managing a dry change of clothes. Have had a hell of a job with the workshop marquee. I'm enclosing five drachma notes, German duds in fact, not worth anything. The value of each one would have been £2500 each. Nubi by the way is Crash's wife, an only child, and I believe is missing her own people (Italian).

We, about twenty of us, went this evening to the 72nd General Hospital for our vaccination. When we got there they hadn't any. The hospital must have OK'd our going – makes me rave and curse. My mum has worked out in her own way when I'm due leave – it would be funny if not so sad. She says her heart is panting for the day. I've just read another Susan Erty book, *Anger in the Sky*, published in 1943. Love always, N.

Air Graph – This must be the last of Norman's air graphs.
18 November 1945

It's eleven days since I heard from you last and ten since mail of any kind, the last being Mum's and Mrs Iveson's. Yesterday I had a telegram from Jack and Mrs A wishing me all the best. So I'm looking forward to a batch, possibly it's because we have moved but we have been static ten days. The weather has been terrible of late and the country an awful wet mess. I'm on guard tonight and will be thinking of you in the small hours as you do me when on nights. Last night I managed to get up to date with some letters, but still more to do yet. It's six weeks since I sent your Xmas parcel, though I don't expect verification just yet. That's all again. All love, N.

Air Mail   18 November 1945

Your letter of 12th, along with my birthday present, arrived yesterday and thanks for all the thoughts conveyed. Glad you got the electricity bill paid for Mum's house – always get rid of debts. With regards to the card you got from Oddfellows just forget it, I'm blowed if I know what it's about. Anyway it says, 'If no reply the amount will be replaced at your funeral expenses.' So that's that. I'll get a better funeral. The weather remains shocking. Today has been a day off but I've had the worst job of all my army career, making a coffin for one of our lads killed in a truck accident with a second in dock with a compound fracture of the skull and a third with lesser injuries and a fourth back at camp with us, suffering from shock. The funeral is to be tomorrow. He has a wife and four kiddies – one he's never seen – poor lassie.

I'm still the 16th in order of leave, dear, and as we have had a good party back from England yesterday we are expecting some allocations early this week. That's all dearest. Bye, N.

Air Mail   **Taranto, Italy**   27 November 1945

So far, so good, presuming my last letter to you was telling you of my leave at last. So to start at the beginning. We left our camp about 10.30 a.m. on Friday morning, the 23rd, and booked in at the transit camp at Athens just before dinner. We were allocated huts, drew palliasse, had tea and bed. Saturday morning had breakfast and prepared to move off and left by train for Pireaus – just after dinner went straight aboard from tenders, had tea and early to bed. Sunday morning we sailed at first light, about 7.00 a.m., and from then on we did a good steady speed. I noted we were on a good sized boat, but apart from rack-type beds the boat was all troopers – bloody lousy! On going to bed on Sunday night we put our watches back one hour, so we are now back on Italian time. We arrived in Taranto Bay sometime early on Tuesday – that's this morning, after a most calm crossing all day Monday. Still Tuesday we disembarked about 11.00 a.m., took trucks to this transit camp, had dinner and now have been given our tent. This is 'BL' too, no bed, straight on deck, so we are hoping it doesn't rain. So you see, dear, our first step is behind us and according to the notice board there is no further ship movement until Thursday. So perhaps then we shall set off for Milan on our second stop. I hope so anyway, for I don't like hanging about and as you will realise it isn't too good in transit and I want so very much to see you. I can't tell you any more about my arrival and unless we are still stuck here for some days this is the last letter you will get before my wire and me. So I'm hoping you get the time off and that you are as happy about this miracle as I am. That's all and all my love, N.

Air Mail   Still at Taranto   30 November 1945

Didn't think I'd be writing again after 27th, having been here since Tuesday. However, this afternoon we are going a bit further and I'm hoping this reaches you before me. Not that it matters greatly if it shouldn't. Our stay here hasn't been too bad for a transit camp, especially so as we are coming on leave when nothing seems too bad. Mind you, we haven't had many comforts. It's still bitterly cold with strong winds. Today, however, is beautiful, no wind, and some glorious sunshine. Since breakfast we paraded at 9.00 a.m. and had yet another FFI (free from infection examination). At eleven we draw our free issue of cigarettes for the day. Then about 3.00 p.m. we parade and march to the station and leave by train about tea-time and arrive after riding some thirty six to forty hours at Milan. Whichever day we arrive we stay the night at Calais and the next day we hope to get home. I can't see me getting home before the 5th and possibly the 8th. So look for my wire and get at least five weeks off. Bye dear, N.

The telegram came and his arrival. The time factor has robbed me of some details, but you may be sure I was there for the greeting. I did get two weeks off. My husbad was able to be his own person, staying at times with his mother and friends. As I finished each of my remaining shift duties he would be there to meet me. I do remember how difficult it was to keep in step with a soldier. I have no qualms but remember it as a happy time and great rejoicing. In my own little bungalow we were as free as air. Came the day when we parted on the station and his return to duty. He was a happier man. The strain of his war service seemed to have vanished and his whole being refreshed and ready to tackle the remaining months until his due demob date.

Returning from Leave

At Navaro, Near Milan   Letter of 9 and 10 January 1946

Just got knocked out at rummy in the NAAFI, so have been writing to Mum and doubt if I'll write to you. It depends if I'm called back into the school.

It was Monday and we were up at 5.30 a.m., had breakfast and handed in blankets, fell in and got on the train, packed like sardines. The windows were in, lights on, but no heating. My feet were so bitterly cold. We got away about 8.00 a.m. and there are about eight to a carriage. I was going to tell you the towns we passed through, dear, but my memory played tricks. However, I do remember Boulogne further down the coast, Amiens, Etaples, Dijon and into Switzerland, Lausanne, Montreaux, St Moritz and Brig, then the Simplon Tunnel of Milan. Switzerland looked grand, you would love a holiday there, I'm confident, so clean, all the fields cultivated, all the trees and hedges trimmed, gardens absolutely in order and the houses so neat and finished off. The mountains are terrific and of course all covered in snow. Seem to go on forever. Miles of Christmas tree forests draped in snow and folks ski-ing down the slopes. Lausanne is beautiful with a terrifically huge lake which had hundreds of different coloured ducks disporting themselves. Massive hotels for the tourists with uniformed attendants in glorious colours and as I've already mentioned, the usual Swiss cleanliness everywhere, making it truly a millionaire's play-ground.

So far, so good, dear. We are still alive and beginning to feel a bit more cheerful – for, believe me, it was a hell of a wrench coming back to it all after a month of paradise, but now we are back in the army and adapting ourselves again. Before coming on leave, we talked of nothing else. Now it's all over, demobbing is the latest topic. Everyone is reckoning on when he will be out and how many more weeks he has to do but, alas, can't make mine before July at the earliest and though I may be wrong, of course, but don't start banking on anything, but won't it be grand when my turn comes at last. I can hardly see to write this, dear, as the light is so bad, it being 5.30 p.m., but I must let you know that a new draught has just gone up and all of us from our unit are on it and we are off to Taranto tonight, parading at 7.30. So I must away and hand in blankets, pack up my kit and generally prepare for the off. That's all dear, will be with you in Taranto. Bye love, N.

Letter **Bari** 13 January 1946

What a funny old army. In my last I think I said we're entraining within the hour for Taranto. Well we got on the train all right, but only on the train for Milan, where we went into transit again. That was Wednesday and it was about midnight when we got bedded down, but I stayed until 12.00 p.m., Thursday dinner time and had twelve good hours in slumberland. At night I saw Lucile Bacan and Humphrey Bogart in *To Have and Have Not*, which was quite good and was in bed by 10.00 p.m. and stayed for another twelve hour stretch. Friday that brings us to, so I had a hair cut, shave and shower, change of clothes and general clean up all round,

198

which was just as well for we set off that same night once again for Taranto. We breakfasted at Rimini, lunched at Ancona and had dinner at Pescara after the first night in the train. We spent the second night with one on each rack, four in the four corners of the carriage and I and another laddie on the carriage floor, plenty of heat for a change this time, but corridor compartment windows missing and outside corridor windows boarded up, so that with no lights it wasn't too good but with good weather ever since reaching Italy it has compensated us somewhat.

That got us over Saturday into Sunday where we breakfasted at Barletta, (it was here that I was in hospital when I had jaundice), and where we were told to detrain at Bari instead of Taranto and so we have, which means of course that we shan't see Taranto and that's just as well for it was lousy in transit there. However, we are in transit now at Bari. In fact, to be precise, we are in the 'air lifts' camp and points towards being flown to Greece – and incidently don't mind which we do, either fly or go by sea. Whichever, expect it will be in a day or two. We have a story quite true, this time from Greece, that one of our field companies are going to Salonika – so we may – but will not know until we get to Greece. We are hoping this isn't so far, it's another two or three days by the most awful roads right up north next to Turkey or alternatively by sea.

The camp is quite good. We are in huts and have hessian beds. There are good latrines, ablutions, showers, cookhouses and dining halls, two cinemas, big NAAFI, wine bar, library, post office, reading room and games room and German POW to do all the fatigues. All we have to do is guard duty if picked and watch no one pinches our kit, which is difficult at times. I think that's all, dear, and I'm away for a shower and to try and feel clean again. So keep happy and smiling. I'm thinking of you always with all my love. N.

Sunday morning and here at Taranto after all. I think I passed rather uncomplimentary remarks about this camp in my last letter – they still hold! Here we have beds of a kind, they are three quarter inch gas piping frames laced across at six inch intervals with electric wire and, as you can imagine, not very comfortable. They do at least keep us off the floor. When laying on my back my heels and shoulders poke through. When laying on my side my hips, elbows and shoulders poke through and it's impossible to lay on my stomach. Anyhow it's better than nothing.

Thursday and ever since for that matter, it has rained most of the time. I did manage to write to Betty and Ted and Dave Holmes. Friday did hardly anything. Saturday. Yesterday we were elated as a boat arrived from Greece bringing release group 25 and of course would take us back. Alas, a lot have gone but not us. Anyway, we hear a boat is due in either today or tomorrow. In this release party I have just spoken of were two of our lads who say we have a new OC, Major Laird hving been released on Class C and has gone back to finish his education at Edinburgh University. Instead of one captain we now have three. Umpteen of the lads have been released under Class A and several through Class B. We shall have a job to recognise the company with so many new faces. That a new division is being formed and we are expected to move into it, then have different strength, different make up of sections and of course be a divisional field park company and no longer a corps field park, all of which is possibly Irish to you. I believe we are to start drilling and playing at soldiers again. Who knows, anything can happen.

We are still at the same place and can, on getting to Greece, be with the company in a few hours. I'm still wondering, of course, what progress, if any, has been made with regard to Aunt's house and the business venture. You will be able to appreciate with what anticipation I'm looking forward to collecting my mail at the company when I get back for it will be about three weeks since leaving you by then. Ever yours, N.

Air Mail   **Taranto**   24 January 1946

Still here and no sign of moving. All movement to Greece frozen. There's a change from field park company to 'divisions'. All transit, reception and movement is so congested and they simply cannot take any more. So here we are, miles from anywhere – nothing to do and can't even take a bath. I've had this same shirt on since I left you on leave – I'm filthy. If there was any sun I could wash my clothes in cold water, but there's no means of drying as it rains every day.

I've written to Aunt about the house too, but with a tenant in it won't be an easy thing. I am stagnating here. My energy, my brain is just being wasted and enough of my life and ours has gone already. You must think I'm a pretty miserable sort, but don't worry about it. If I've made you feel blue – sorry, I don't mean to. Cheer up and attend to all you can at your end. By the way, I have written to Jack and Mrs A and I've got one pipe for Ted. Keep happy. Love, N.

Letter   30 January 1946

Back at last. Use this address for the time being: 2160917 L/Cpl Bell N, 258 Field Park Coy, RE, CMF. We came back here in time for tea last night. There were many letters waiting, three from Mum and yours of 19, 20 and 24 November (last year!), there were also yours of 9, 17 and 19 January and then today I received yours of 25 January. Before I answer I think I ought to finish my travels back to the company.

After writing to you last on 24 January, we were detailed to leave the next day but it was cancelled for twenty four hours. However, we did get away on the 26th and sailed about 2.00 p.m. What an awful tub. It had only been built this war. A utility type, if ships are that way. It did everything bar sink, pitch roll and even jump and all normal tricks. Most of us were sick, although I wasn't but felt pretty rotten. As we had run into a stinking storm it took three days instead of thirty six hours. We were all fed up. However, we disembarked about dinner time and as I've said arrived back here about tea time. All kinds of new things have happened and hundreds of new faces. We are a completely new section, but keep writing to the same address and I will let you know of any change, as there's bound to be some slight differences. Before I forget, Crash asked me to send you apologies for not writing whilst on compassionate leave, his wife had flu. His mother's illness is serious and he is trying to get a home posting or out on Class B. His wife is expecting the baby in March and it seems 'the flu' was quite a new experience to her, but she is happy. Aunt's letter seems OK and your reply perfect. All in order so far. Contact Jackson about the house situation. He may be able to help if anyone can. All love, N.

Air Mail   3 February 1946

Since writing to you last I have had my first taste of work again and at night on guard was able to write a few lines to friends before the fun started – men being absent from camp. I spent much time walking round billets checking them in. The next day fourteen were on charge, so I'd another do giving evidence and I guess making enemies. The next day I was a witness at a court of enquiry. So all in all I've had enough of marching in and out of orderly rooms for the rest of my duration in the army. Yesterday, Saturday, we finished works at dinner time and played REME workshops at football in the afternoon, just managing to win 1-0, and I'm stiff today.

I have had the entire day off and stayed in bed until 10.00 a.m. I did a bit of darning, had dinner, a nap and written to Mum. It's gloriously sunny and fairly warm. The last leave party has just got back. Two went yesterday on B release, one being 'Cosher', the Sheffield lad whom you met on the station when we were returning from leave. Longing to hear from you. All love, N.

Air Mail   7 February 1946

On guard again tonight and hoping for a quieter one than last time. Had your letter of the 29th the other day. Your few kind words are encouraging and it's good to know you understand. You would breathe a sigh of relief to know there are two briar pipes for Ted. Poor efforts, but the best I could do. I haven't had any news about the business venture from JA and no news from you about the house you are trying to sort out for us. We do so need something in the interval before being able to build our own. I've five men on the beat so must go round and have a look at them. Bye love, N.

Air Mail   15 February 1946

I'm always groaning about my need for your letters and now have the ones of the 5th and 8th. I'm pleased you are getting mail from me more easily and your worries lessened. A delay of ten days seems like a lifetime when there is a long gap. It may be due to the bad weather. The last two days were unspeakable. The mountains are covered with snow and the wind howling and blowing powdery snow. It has been so cold in bed. What does make me ponder and smile is that in spite of the cold, all the orange trees are laden with fruit. I was very irked when I got the letter and refusal of the house. Your reply was quite good indeed, smashing. How rotten your weather is too. It must be very unpleasant chasing up and down that ruddy great hill and these letters to write about business and the general hurry and worry of the same. So remember I'm thinking of you.

My leave seems now at times to have been such a brief interlude. Then I so distinctly remember and ache to recall them. I'm sure, dear, you must be bankrupt each week. I'm trying not to spend but finally had to as I was owing cash and simply could not bear it. We have been asked not to send flowers at this time of year, as it takes six weeks to make arrangements. It's a great disappointment for me with your birthday nearing. Have you received the bedside lamp I made for you? Time is getting on and I must have a warm up and bit of supper. All love, N.

Letter   19 February 1946

Just the job – two letters from you today. You will note the new address: 17th Electrical and Mechanical Platoon, attached to 258 Divisional Field Park Company, Royal Engineers, CMF, but you can abbreviate it. A newly formed 13 Division which has as its sign a black horse shoe on a red ground. We are just Land Forces Greek Troops now. Our sign is a Greek fig leaf on a white ground.

Sorry to hear about Fred D's illness. Yes, I knew of him and his wife. You had a letter from him whilst I was on leave. Thanks for taking my coat to the cleaners. How's my suits – either of them any moths? Must think of another house, even though it will set us back a few years. We need somewhere if it's only a refuge from relatives and other earthly pests. I've heard from J and Mrs A. but nothing about business. All love, N.

Letter   27 February 1946

I received your letter of the 23rd in five days. Alas, the news
about that woman and her latest attitude towards you in her
letter. I'm not in a fit state to write I'm so angry. What you
did was by our solicitor's advice. Aunt had tried and stood
to do well out of the deal and was willing. Forget it. Hope
we get chance of some other place and concentrate on
establishing our own as soon as possible. About my insurance.
Close payments; it's half of what I get daily in the army. I've
sent off a sponge and mixed dried fruit to B and T and similar
to Mrs A. for her kindness and interest to us. A parcel will
get to you as soon as I can manage it. Don't worry, dear,
whatever the outcome of our plans, I'll understand. Keep
happy and smiling. Love, N.

Letter   5 March 1946

I've received your letter of 27 February. Now I feel I must
get written in time for your next birthday. Sending my dearest
wishes to you and the hope that next year I'll be with you
for the occasion. Glad to know the parcel is on the way to
me at last. I secretly wondered why it had taken you so long.
I know full well you have had so much on. I've no idea how
Mum is managing her income. If she had £10 a week she
would spend it and has no value of money. We have lots more
new faces this week, a new OC, lance sergeant, three corporals,
four or five lance corporals, so my hope of promotion goes
once again. Happy days. Love, N.

Air Mail   9 March 1946

We've had no post into Greece since the 6th, due it is said,
to bad flying weather. I'm not grumbling as I'd two of your

letters in hand. So all's right with the world. You've had the business venture news a day before me. I've written to J and Mrs A. and now I'm contemplating getting out on Class B, if J can arrange it for me. The first batch of 27s have gone on release. I'm now group 10, every day means one day nearer, but, alas, I shall miss another summer. Did you have a nice birthday and incidentally when is it my Mum's!? Love always, N.

Letter   13 March 1946

I've your letters of 2nd, 3rd, and 5th to answer and will try and work through them. As yet I haven't heard from J. or Mrs A. and presume that all is going ahead. In fact, you tell me most of what I know about the business and I'm wondering who the team will be. You say they're going to ask me to apply for my B release. The firm has to apply through the Ministry of Labour with an application form and not from me. Have you had at least two more parcels from me? I haven't told Mum about this business as it may get round and do harm. Love, N.

Air Mail   17 March 1946

Mail is bad again. In fifteen days a brief note from Mrs A. says the licence has come through. I feel I'm being left out but as it's your monthly visit I expect you will be telling me something as soon as you get home again. Things are so vague and prolonged, my appetite for the cause is ravenous. I'm afraid I over did it with the 27s on the eve of their release and was pretty rough the next day. I was on guard the following twenty four hours. Part guarding a prisoner, but was later able to make up the sleep loss. Have had today off, it being Sunday. It's cold and windy but we have a good fire and I'm shortly to fry an egg and then retire for a good night's sleep. See you one fine day. As always, my love, N.

Air Graph   24 March 1946

Just dressed after an intersection match and won 3-0 and I'm writing this before anything else. Your latest of 15 March and no parcel has arrived for you. I'm sorry after all my saving for the right day – dash it all. I'm not in a position to get anything for Mum but will write to her. I don't see why the Ministry of Labour want to see you. After all you are on a job of importance, if not national. Let me know what transpires. Everything fine over here. Keep happy. Bye love, N.

Air Mail   25 March 1946

Will you remind me of Mum's birthday once again? I've had a letter from B and T today and yours of the 17th whilst on your weekend. I can well imagine the excitement and news in the village now it's around and that J. and K. have made a start. I've had a letter from K. who says he has met you. He is a very clever chap and competent. I feel we three can make a go of it and it will help with the old trailer I made and converted when in the period of rescue at the first aid post prior to my call up and Ken's car is to be used. Young Ken is in dock; I hope it doesn't interfere with his release. It is good to know work is coming in. I'm biding my time as patiently as I can. All love, N.

Letter   26 March 1946

In the last two days I've had letters from J. and Mrs A. and Mum. Yours of the 10th, 11th and 12th, for which thanks very much. The lights have been out for an hour but now back on and hoping they will stay. It's a standing joke with the lads about promotions and are stupified too at the way in which they are carried out. I haven't written to Beverley yet about the plot, not being in the mood at present. B. and T. never seem able to do enough for me they have been very kind and Ted appreciates the pipes. The lights have gone again and it's now the next day and your parcel had arrived with toothpaste, envelopes, Bovril and ingrams. Have had a smashing shave for a change. Glad you have now got parcels 1 and 2. The victory service was at Headquarters and couldn't all attend so had our own with leaflets issued. Until next time. All my love, N.

Letter   28 March 1946

Please note we're now 'British Forces in Greece', not CMF. So you have made the contribution to the business – which now makes the three of us square and I'm now a fully fledged partner. Thanks for the figures quoted as also from our joint bank account. It's a damned good show on your part. I've despatched some more odds and ends and sponges off to you. We get sponges freely and cheaply here. I'm out of aspirins. I'd saved some when medical orderly and they often kid away a headache, so would you please send me some when you make up another parcel. After a week of scorching weather in which nearly everyone turned red, today and during the nights is very cold and rainy. So it's not very pleasant. Last night we had a truck pinched and now more men on guard. We've been given a lecture and told off for not carrying out our duties properly – this from the 'Guard Commanders'. It means we have to be lousy so and sos with the lads. I'm simply more fed up than usual. Never mind, don't listen to my grumbling. My love to you alone. N.

Air Mail   31 March 1946

Mail in general is not good with us. So do hope mine is reaching you. I have yours of the 23rd. It is possibly due this last few weeks because of the growing tension of the Greek elections taking place today and for which we have been confined to camp since last night and all packed and ready for any emergency or trouble. I'm sorry if I am showing that I may be melancholic, it certainly isn't aimed at you. You have every right to feel the same, as you have certainly got through some work lately for our joint benefits. All love, dear, N.

Letter   4 April 1946

Haven't heard from you for a week, yet I've had two from Mum. It may be that she is using the old address and you the new one. I worry in case you are ill or something. My time at the moment is having two chaps for training and another five on Monday. So I'm watching and instructing their respective efforts. According to our wireless and our service papers, you are having a good spell of weather. Do hope you are able to enjoy it and the open moors. Our 28s are awaiting to move off any day.

The elections went off very well. Some slight disturbances – a couple of British lads wounded. We were all on guard at different places in case. Apart from menancing looks and during the night some arms fire, nothing untoward happened to us. You never know with these folk. One section wants us out of Greece, yet another section do not, as they fear when we go all semblance of order will go too, also work and food. I'm always longing for your letters and wondering how you are faring, eating enough and getting enough rest or recreation. My love to you. N.

Air Mail   13 April 1946

It seems it will take as long to get me out on B release as wait for my demob. All this coming from my partners. Our service newspaper says Isaacs would be making a speech and giving out group numbers for demob for up to September. I'm almost sure to be in the list. That's all, write as often as you can. Young Ken is on his way out, also Crash. He says his wife is due for the baby now. All love, N.

Letter   15 April 1946

Yesterday was a veritable red letter day, one from my mum, two from you and one from one of the demobbed lads. Today I receive one from Mrs A. Where on earth did you get a typewriter from?

I marvel at your capabilities. Most intriguing and as you say only a few mistakes. We now have the best news ever from a business point of view and each day brings me closer to you. Lovely days are ahead. B. and T.'s wish has come true at last. (A longed for baby). Ken B. writes to say that arrangements are going through and has sent for signature and given me other information. It seems housing us is now the priority. N.

Letter   22 April 1946

Received your letter of the 10th two days ago in which you told of your flying visit to Mum. Then one of the 16th saying you had been gathering bluebells. Always a lovely thought comes to mind. I am enclosing a snap, which has just come to light, of the old company team before the lads started going home on demob. This taken at Rivigo, south of the River Po and Adize, where we played the Italian team in their stadium. There's Ginger H. whose girl, Etta, you corresponded with once. I'm glad that all the parcels I've sent are now accounted for, in spite of worries of having gone astray. This service has been very, very good, in spite of what seemed hits and misses at times. The work you have all put in your respective spheres leaves me amazed. We are back on mepacrine tablets and they are horrible. Mrs A. is certainly one on a thousand; like you I deeply appreciate her. She is always feeding and looking after the works. Yes, definite news has been released of the demob group. Mine works out at 5 September, so that's encouraging. All love, N.

Air Mail   26 April 1946

The jolly old mail is scarce again, but I've had your parcel with aspirin and toothpaste. Many thanks. We are expecting the GOC (General Officer Commanding) to visit us any day. Instead of getting on with our work we have been blancoing everything, whitewashing and generally squaring up and wasting time, not to mention rehearsals of drill. We actually stood on parade for an hour and a half on Wednesday afternoon, much to our disgust and discomfort. It seems so futile, I can't for the life of me understand full grown men being treated like this. You might mention it to your MO and see what his reactions are as an ex-officer. Who was the woman you introduced to me who said she liked to see soldiers covered in Blanco? Only those who have to do it know the revulsion it creates. This is how the British army carries on in peace-time. Sorry to be belly aching. My diary says sixteen weeks to release. All love, N.

Letter   30 April 1946

I received your two letters of 22nd March this morning, the first mail for a week and I was eager to read them. No letters of any description from elsewhere. So you are to have a break in Bridlington. Just now I'm afraid I've lost interest of any kind and have let the correspondence go. I had to give up the chance of learning to drive with the Motor Transport as I'd too much work on and no one to take my place, etc., but they will have to part with me one day. Would you try and get a Mitchell's *Constructing Book on Building*. I've managed to skip through one and it has some useful stuff in for me. Crash had a wire today and learnt that he has a son. At the moment Mum is at Chester, Aunt Maggie is ill. Mum had written a letter to you and must have left it behind at home and asked if I would tell you. Only a few more months dear, to love and beauty, bless you. N.

Letter   4 May 1946

Before I forget can you possibly get me another book?! *The Handyman's Complete Instructor*, published by Oldhams press. Quite the most interesting book I've come across. Our 28s go on Monday. Crash is one of them – that's another old mate I'm losing. He is longing to see his wife and son. He had been in the army six and a half years – a blooming long time. A letter from Mum in Chester says she found her letter to you in her handbag. As a penance for forgetting Mum's birthday, she has asked for a handbag, so I'm drawing some money to do so and will get one for you and I'll be delighted if you like it. Will be going into Athens tonight for the second time since being back. Since dinner have washed my overalls in petrol, had a shower and written this, so must wind up. All love, N.

Letter 15 May 1946

Have I mentioned that we are British Forces in Greece? We have moved on again today, quite good billets in a private house, but I'm afraid other than that not too happy – enough said. We are awakened at 5.30 a.m., breakfast at 6.15 a.m., first parade at 7.00 a.m., lunch between 11 and 12.00 p.m., finishing work at 3.00 p.m. and lights out at 11.00 p.m. On my demob I should get £2 17s. 9d. (£2.89) per week plus a weekly food ration of £1 4s. 0d. (£1.20) plus your money of £1 19s. 0d. (£1.95), which will help us out somewhat. See you love, N.

Letter 19 May 1946

Your letter of the 11th arrived yesterday along with one from Mum from Chester, but she will be back home now. She says you have invited her, along with your mum to go on the holiday, but will be refusing as she cannot let you pay. I'd just like to say thanks. The 29s of this new parent company are leaving for home tomorrow. Yet our 258 company 30s left today, which makes it very complicated to work out. George H., my old work mate in 258, has had to go and leave me in this last group, so we all had our farewell drink last night. To wash overalls in petrol is quite simply that the oil and grease falls away after a short soaking and after being hung out in the strong sunshine for a couple of hours there's no smell and lovely and clean. I should have two sets of everything in the clothing line at home at least. The army supplies an issue of clothing on demob, but as yet don't know what. I do expect a clothing and food allowance. I've got another book from this company's library which I must have. Do try and get it for me. It's *Woodcraft in Design and Practice* by Rodney Hooper, publisher BT Batsford. You will notice that I'm Corporal – I was offered sergeant's tapes but refused. I didn't want to leave the lads at this stage, so a regular has been made up. It will do him more good than me. All love and happy days, N.

213

Letter 23 May 1946

Heard from Mum today and J. and Mrs A. She had enclosed two sprays of wallflowers and they smelt lovely. You could if you wished tell your MO that I am almost opposite the 72 General Hospital here at which he once told me he was on the staff and on the road to Glafarden. It gets warmer every day and I work stripped to the waist and spend practically all our spare time off sunbathing and swimming. Since moving here, we have been building a large workshop and it is just about finished, so should in about a week's time be under way with normal work again, but Lord it is hot working. All love, N.

Letter 27 May 1946

Had your letter of the 20th yesterday, the first at our new address. After two days of very stormy weather, heavy seas, rain showers and fitful sunshine we appear to be getting back to normal. Blazing sunny stuff, quite calm tonight and every sign of a good day tomorrow. It's a drag getting up at 5.30 a.m. We are an hour in front of British Summer time, but we can manage a swim, wash and change with knocking off at 3.00 p.m. Another rise next week, for fourth year increment, so should be able to live for a few weeks when I'm home. These weeks are sadly dragging themselves out. All love, N.

Letter 4 June 1946

It is possible that a letter written to you on the 31st May could have been destroyed in the plane which caught fire and all mail lost. Good egg! Your letters of the 28 and 29 May arrived today and like you, I was wanting a letter. Perhaps I'm just greedy. I'd no idea cigarettes with you were in short supply. It may be due to the curtailing of American supplies. We have no shortage in our rations but they are of all kinds and some old and unsmokable. Your new medical department is open, so will you be sharing service in both? Mother told me in her last letter that you will be going for the weekend and that you will be rushed. I know you have to be tactful in going to see Mrs A. whilst there, but hope you can manage it and glean more for us both. I've been in the army four years today and getting a few more coppers. Yes, I do remember the early days when I was horrid to you and you stamped on my bad foot. All love, N.

Letter   8 June 1946

I've got your letter of 30 May to hand. It's *Victory Day* today and we have had it off and as it's Whit Monday tomorrow we've got that off too. Rumour has it that we shall have Thursday off as it's the King's birthday. In that case I've no excuse for not writing. Glad the mats and lamp have arrived. Pleased you managed the money side by writing to the paymaster. It will be quicker for you and easier for me. I've reckoned up cash that isn't yet credited to me and several items not through from the paymaster. Fancy you giggling at your MO's remarks and at your age too! Take it easy. All love, N.

Letter   12 June 1946

No mail from you again. We were warned there would not be any mail for two days because of the victory celebrations and though we had the days off, I'd rather have your letters. We have tomorrow off for the King's birthday. Peacetime soldiers always have it off.

Will you send me at your earliest possible moment another jar of Ingrams and tube of MacLeans. I'd hoped to manage but what I can buy is awful stuff. Thanks a lot. It is still boiling hot and the locals say July is hotter. One sweats and sweats until 3.00 p.m. when we all just fall in the sea and breathe again. Oh, they tell me August is the peak heat. If that is so I'll be little more than a skeleton by my turn for transit. Our food though not too bad, but it isn't what I'd have normally for this weather. We don't seem to get fresh vegetables, salad things or fruit. I can't eat my lunch or dinner and find myself buying eggs and chips and salads in the evening. In fact that seems to be where all my money goes, but I don't begrudge it. I'd a letter from Crash the other day, and he tells me how good it is to be back in civvy street. His son weighed 9 1/2 lbs at birth, a perfect blond, and has been eating and sleeping ever since Crash got home. So the baby seems to have all his father's habits. Crash was a great lad. I love you, N.

Letter   16 June 1946

I have been having my teeth seen by the dentist and there's three for filling. The dental officer is only young and soon going on release. He's from the 72nd General Hospital and very good. One of our chaps, whilst diving, struck a hard substance on the bottom and is now in the above hospital with a broken neck, is in plaster from waist to ears and being flown home shortly. I'm to have my last inoculation in the army. I don't feel too good to start with – it's this dreadful heat I think, amongst other things. However, please accept my groaning once more. Love you, N.

Letter   20 June 1946

I have received your letters of 12 and 13 June. I never have
real cause to grumble – they turn up in the end. The Lord
only knows why mine take so long reaching you. There's mail
from B. and T. and Mrs A. Being a corporal has its setbacks,
although on the whole I'm much better off. I was approached
by the OC to take charge of a big new workshop employing
solely Greek labour and with the offer of my third stripe and
bomb to follow shortly after, but of course, there was a snag
– six months deferment of my release. So I had no other
thought than that of refusing. What does that tell you, as it
did me? I've sent off a parcel to your mum and dad and one
for you. No, you didn't tell me why you didn't get over to
Mum's but I now understand. We seem to be having a hold-up
with shipping here. Some lads are overdue by several days on
their demob. I got a bit of news from Mrs A. She says how
bad the rations are and sure they have been eating horsemeat.
I'm sure she has a bit o'bacon boiling, I can smell it and can
nearly taste it! She says the firm, amongst many things, has
thirty seven lavatories to alter. Well it's starters! Fancy Mrs
A. says there's a shortage of matches too. As ever, N.

Letter   24 June 1946

I've received your short note on arrival at Bridlington.

Enclosed you will find five snaps, taken last week, of our
billets. One is from the sea and shows our room, from which
I am now writing. You will notice the wide balcony and in
the foreground our raft made from four oil drums, two
bedsteads and some timber which we anchor out for diving
off. The next is a snap of a Coles Crane in the background.
Incidently the workshop is fifty feet long and built in a week.
Next is a close up of Lofty Langford on his lathe. Fourth, the
blacksmith's shop with Corporal Bourne, J. Neary, Ted Heley

and Arthur Bailey doing their stuff. Lastly the group with me back from leave. I did tell you that I'd sent your folk some sponges and a tin of crayfish, which we can get in abundance at our canteen. So will be sending you something of that nature. It will help rations out a bit. No more groups out as there hasn't been a boat for a week. It will soon be my turn to board the lugger. Hoping to hear from you soon. All love, N.

Letter   28 June 1946

Yesterday I had your last letter from Bridlington and the long lovely letter after your return home, for which I love you lots. It has heartened me tremendously. So pleased you enjoyed it and the good weather. Do you know I've forgotten entirely about feeling ill, but feel rotten for having mentioned it. You are my confidant and I suppose I appease myself in relating my bits of piffle and gripes. I'm awaiting Ken's letter and agreement to sign. I understand building materials are difficult to get just now. Seems they are stuck for a joiner and I could be so useful. I'm sending a parcel soon. Once more my love, N.

Letter   2 July 1946

Had a letter from your mum and dad yesterday and one from you of 23 June. The chap who had a suspected broken neck is now walking about, and still in plaster, and has been flown home. He was in a happy state of mind the evening before his flight. I'm trying to last out on my last pen nib. Have managed to send your folk some cigarettes and chocolate. To you the long promised handbag in which you will find some tablets of soap. It is smashing for cleaning but runs away at a fair rate. We have had bacon croquettes sometimes and just the job to make the ration go further. I'll enquire of the cooks for the recipe for you. Nothing further to add, but my love, N.

Letter 6 July 1946

I've heard from the business side twice from Ken and one of his previous ones missing according to what I've learned. This has been the problem, I'd thought I was being neglected when all the time it was the hit and miss of postal services. It seems all is going well and jobs coming in. In between times they are building me a Nissen hut, the type used by the army. Today I'd a letter from Mum saying you have had to cancel your visit due to a change in shifts. She seems to think industrial nursing more tying than hospital. She was somewhat disappointed as she wanted to discuss arrangements for when I'm demobbed. I've sent a letter off to the Ministry of Works in London asking for approved small house and particulars to be sent home. It's worth a try. I'm hoping to send off another parcel with some odds and ends I'm eliminating. Bailey has gone through the ritual and ready for home. I'm rather expecting that next week I'll be having my medicals, which brings the happy day nearer. In fact six weeks and I set sail for Valhalla. Get my letters answered. Yours, N.

Letter 14 July 1946

Sunday evening and just had tea, been for the mail which hasn't materialised and I've picked up orders at the same time. I've sent off the last parcel to date. I do have your letter of the 5th. The blinking release is going very slowly. Some will be behind their demob date and the Lord knows what will have happened by mine, so I'm anticipating being late. As soon as September is in I'm due for Phython, which is long overseas service leave and which will be tacked on to my other. We have got stacks of reinforcements from England in and who haven't been in the army five minutes, poor beggars. As always, N.

Letter   18 July 1946

Your letter of the 10th arrived last night. I am just recuperating
from the heat and toil of the day. There's another parcel
packed up ready for me to send off to you. Glad you took
Mrs T. something in appreciation of looking after my insurance. Have you made any arrangements for withdrawing –
am I to get it on my return? The cook is in jankers so doubt
if I'll get the bacon recipe now. Anything I send in future will
be to Mum's home. It looks as though we are due out 18
August and 2 September. It only means you will be at Mum's
a little longer and though that is a major calamity, I think
we can survive it. No toothpaste and shaving cream has arrived
yet. Tonight we have Bing Crosby and Bob Hope in *Road to
Utopia* in our canteen. I'm dry – in fact almost dehydrated,
and could drink a small barrel full. Dare I say I could be
home very soon. All love, N.

Letter   22 July 1946

Had a letter today from one of my demobbed mates, Mrs A.
and your mum and dad, who all report the shortages of most
of everything. I'm on guard tonight and sweating cobs from
the oppressive heat. A letter from Crash reports all is well.
Mum has proposed that she goes away for three months once
she has received me home and has suggested financial arrangements. I would advise you not to write me again as the
36s are off, then me. I shall be pining for letters and wish they
were still coming, but it's not advisable really. I'll write from
the different transit camps. We are getting nearer to Glory.
As ever, N.

Letter   26 July 1946

In answering your long letter of 18 July, I'll be happy to know if you have received the handbag. We should have quite a few of those natural sponges that I've managed to send over a long period. I'd no idea we had managed to save the amount you quoted and quite substantial under the circumstances. How the world changes – just over a year ago the preceding last six years we have been fighting a bitter struggle with the Germans. Last week the area commander issued orders that we were to mix with the German prisoners of war, who work with us and to entertain them. Last night saw us all laughing, jabbering and supping together plus playing the usual pub-cum-club games. But dare I say that for all their sins, and God knows how many, I find them very nice chaps, looking like us, wearing our clothes, happy, contented and hard workers. The world will never be right until we all get on together.

I might be able to send off to you some currants and raisins. They will do for Christmas if nothing else.

Nearer the day. All love, N.

The fruit arrived and was the basis of a cake for the home-coming.

Letter   30 July 1946

I'm happy indeed that you have received more mail from me and that the boxes and parcels have arrived and that the handbag has also finally arrived. Your comments gave me great pleasure. Carry on paying my insurance, it may benefit, though I'm not keen on paying insurances. By now we are getting browned off – this drawn-out demob is tantalising. I am feeling sorry for the regulars. All love, N.

Letter   **Kalamata, Greece**   3 August 1946

The address book arrived today and I have been filling it in. There's another parcel of bits and pieces on the way with this brief note, but sending a separate note to say so.

And so it seemed that my husband was on his way home and would appear rather rushed. Kalamata, a port on the west side of Greece, was where the last parcel and note was posted, or so it would seem. I wasn't to hear anything more until 21 August and a telegram from King's Cross in London was delivered, saying 'Arriving 9.22 pm', timed at 2.03 p.m. I think I almost stopped breathing with the tension and trying to contain it. I've never experienced the feeling since and hope never to. The train was on time and the smartest lad in the army leapt out, looking so fit and sunburned, or was he still showing the effects of mepacrine. I remember so vividly the month of August whilst awaiting the homecoming. The days and days of August, when the sky was filled with skein after skein of wild geese going south across the River Humber was a magnificent sight. The weather of that winter and into 1947 was atrocious. The river froze and was covered with icefloes. Starving pigeons stripped the allotments and gardens of Brussel sprouts and cabbages until they were finally shot and we had a few good pigeon pies.

Norman's mum and I had provided a table fit for a king with nothing spared. I think we had lived on bread and jam whilst saving our meagre rations for the occasion. I had managed to travel some ninety miles very carefully with the cake, which was iced and had the shape of a crown on top, done by an expert at my place of work. The very next day he was at work with the firm and although the same day he gouged a three inch wound in his leg with a chisel from his tool bag, it was of no consequence to him – he was home and happy and in work.

Incidentally I still have the Thanksgiving Service leaflet of the First Army for the victory granted to the Allies in North Africa and also that of the Eighth Army.

222

EPILOGUE

On my husband's last leave before being demobbed he had been able to arrange to go into partnership with two mature, trained builders. Once Norman was home accommodation was difficult to find but we did discover a flat, sharing amenities with changing, suspect couples!

We applied to the borough council for planning permission to build on the third of an acre we had bought during 1941 – at the price of £189.00. It was to be three years before we got the go-ahead and our firm had it as their first big job. Restrictions on building materials meant they were still in short supply, particularly wood, so the building area plans had to be made for extension in the future. Ground floors were of concrete, skirting and window ledges of four inch tiles – even the upstairs window ledges – and the narrowest of wood in the skirting boards. We were happy to get into our own home, even though the electricity supply had yet to be connected and furnishing took many years.

At least a decade passed in strife and straining, trials, tribulations, ups and downs, and shortages of practically everything, including money. But at last we realised our dreams.

Cynthia C. Bell

ACKNOWLEDGEMENTS

I am indebted to the following people, with many thanks for their help:

J.G.W. Roberts M.A., DMS, ALA, MILAM
Miss P.J. Martin B.A., ALA
Mary McGarry M.A.
Mrs. Gillian Holmes
Doctor A.H. Stamp M.A., PHD

APPENDIX

Order of Service for the Eighth Army
Service of Thanksgiving

THE NATIONAL ANTHEM

THE BIDDING

We are met together on this memorable day, in the presence of God, with a three-fold desire in our hearts.

First, we desire to approach God, the Creator of the universe, in humility and lowly reverence, with due confession of failure and sin.

Second, we desire to pour out our hearts in fervent thanksgiving to our Father in Heaven, for His great goodness to us in the time of this war.

Third, we desire to dedicate ourselves afresh to His service that we may be found worthy fellow workers with Him in His Kingdom on earth.

WORSHIP

O Worship the King
All glorious above;
O gratefully sing
His power and His love;
Our shield and defender,
The ancient of days.
Pavilioned in splendour,
And girded with praise.

Frail children of dust
And feeble as frail,
In Thee do we trust,
Nor find Thee to fail;
Thy mercies how tender,
How firm to the end!
Our Maker, Defender,
Redeemer and Friend.

O tell of His might,
O sing of His grace,
Whose robe is the Light,
Whose canopy space,
His chariots of wrath
The deep thunder clouds form,
And dark is His path
On the wings of the storm.

O Measureless Might
Ineffable Love,
While angels delight
To hymn Thee above,
Thy humbler creation,
Though feeble their lays
With true adoration
Shall sing to Thy praise.   Amen.

ALL KNEEL

PENITENCE

Chaplain and Congregation :

O God our Father, we have sinned against Thee in thought, word and deed: We have not loved Thee with all our hearts: We have not loved our neighbours as ourselves. Have mercy upon us we beseech Thee: Cleanse us from our sins: and help us to overcome our faults; Through Jesus Christ our Lord. Amen.

Chaplain :

May the Lord Almighty have mercy upon us, forgive us our sins, and bring us to everlasting life: Through Jesus Christ our Lord. Amen.

THE LORD'S PRAYER

THANKSGIVING

HYMN

Now thank we all our God
With heart and hands and voices,
Who wondrous things hath done,
In Whom His world rejoices,
Who from our mother's arms
Hath blessed us on our way
With countless gifts of love,
And still is ours today.

O may this bounteous God
Through all our life be near us,
With ever-joyful hearts
And blessed peace to cheer us,
And keep us in His grace,
And guide us when perplexed,
And free us from all ills
In this world and the next.

226

All praise and thanks to God
The Father now be given,
The Son, and Him who reigns
With Them in Highest Heaven,

The One Eternal God,
Whom earth and heaven adore;
For thus it was, is now,
And shall be evermore.   Amen.

THE LESSON
Revelation 21, verses 1-7.

PRAYERS
Let us pray for the King and his Ministers, his People and his Allies.

O MOST MIGHTY and most merciful Father, the sure stronghold of them that trust in Thee. We remember before Thee our Sovereign Lord, King George, his Ministers, his Forces, his People and his Allies. Contending as one for the liberties of all; that in the strong assurance of Thy heavenly help we may continue to serve Thee and restore to all nations the kindly blessings of peace: Through Jesus Christ our Lord. Amen.

Let us pray for our own homes.

O LORD JESUS CHRIST who didst dwell for thirty years in an earthly home at Nazareth, let Thy Holy Spirit dwell in the hearts of all who dwell in our homes and those whom we love. Keep them in all times of temptation and danger, whenever they are anxious or perplexed or afraid. Hasten the day when we shall be re-united with them with the touch of hand and fellowship. And grant while we are absent from each other we may do nothing that is unworthy of our affection or disloyal to our love, so that when we meet again, we may meet unashamed and go on to build our homes on earth so that we all may be found worthy to be made members of Thy home in Heaven: Through Jesus Christ our Lord. Amen.

Let us pray for those who mourn.

Grant, O Lord, to all who are bereaved the spirit of faith and courage, that they may have strength to meet the days to come with steadfastness and patience; not sorrowing as those without hope, but in thankful remembrance of Thy mercies in past years and in sure expectation of a joyful reunion in Thy heavenly places: Through Jesus Christ our Lord. Amen.

Remembrance of the fallen :

O ETERNAL LORD GOD, who holdeth all souls in life: We beseech Thee to shed forth upon Thy Holy Church in paradise and on earth, the bright beams of Thy light and heavenly comfort; and grant that we, following the good example of those who have lived and served Thee here on earth, and who have laid down their lives, may, at last, enter with Thee into the fullness of Thine unending joy: Through Jesus Christ our Lord. Amen.

A GENERAL THANKSGIVING
Chaplain and congregation :

Almighty God, Father of all mercies, we, Thine unworthy servants, do give Thee most humble and hearty thanks for all Thy goodness and loving-kindness to us, and to all men; We bless Thee for our creation, preservation, and all the blessings of this life: but above all, for Thine inestimable love in the redemption of the world by our Lord Jesus Christ; for the means of grace and for the hope of glory. And, we beseech Thee, give us that due sense of all Thy mercies, that our hearts may be unfeignedly thankful, and that we shew forth Thy praise, not only with our lips, but in our lives; by giving up ourselves to Thy service, and by walking before Thee in holiness and righteousness all our days; through Jesus Christ our Lord, to whom with Thee and the Holy Ghost be all honour and glory, world without end. Amen.

Chaplain :

The grace of our Lord Jesus Christ and the love of God and the fellowship of the Holy Ghost be with us all evermore. Amen.

HYMN

O God, our help in ages past,
Our hope for years to come,
Our shelter from the stormy blast,
And our eternal home.

Beneath the shadow of Thy Throne
Thy saints have dwelt secure;
Sufficient is Thine arm alone,
And our defence is sure.

Before the hills in order stood,
Or earth received her frame,
From everlasting Thou art God,
To endless years the same.

O God, our help in ages past,
Our hope for years to come,
Be Thou our guard while troubles
last,
And our eternal home.   Amen.

ADDRESS

HYMN

God of our fathers, known of old,
Lord of our far-flung battle-line,
Beneath whose awful hand we hold
Dominion over palm and pine —
Lord God of Hosts be with us yet,
Lest we forget — lest we forget!

The tumult and the shouting dies;
The captains and the kings depart;
Still stands Thine ancient sacrifice,
An humble and a contrite heart.
Lord God of Hosts, be with us yet,
Lest we forget — lest we forget!

Far-called, our navies melt away,
On dune and headland sinks the fire;
Lo, all our pomp of yesterday
Is one with Nineveh and Tyre!
Judge of the Nations, spare us yet,
Lest we forget — lest we forget!

For heathen heart that puts her trust
In reeking tube and iron shard,
All valiant dust that builds on dust,
And guarding, calls not Thee to guard,
For frantic boast and foolish word —
Thy mercy on Thy people, Lord!
                                Amen.

LET US PRAY FOR THE PEACE MAKERS

Eternal God, wonderful in counsel, excellent in wisdom, we pray for the representatives of the nations who are called to the task of laying the foundations of peace and of settling the affairs of this distracted and embittered world. Inspire their minds, enlarge their vision, direct their councils, that humble and wise, fearless and unfaltering, they may stand for righteousness and truth. We pray also for the peoples in whose name they speak; raise the minds of men everywhere above the mists of suspicion and hatred into the pure light of justice and goodwill, that justice and freedom may be established among all nations: through Jesus Christ our Lord. Amen.

ACT OF DEDICATION

Chaplain and congregation :

Teach us, good Lord, to serve Thee as Thou deservest;
To give and not to count the cost;
To fight and not to heed the wounds;
To toil and not to seek for rest;
To labour and not to ask for any reward save that of knowing that we do Thy will;
Through Jesus Christ our Lord. Amen.

THE CHARGE

Go forth into the world in peace; be of good courage; hold fast that which is good; render to no man evil for evil; strengthen the faint-hearted; support the weak; help the afflicted; honour all men; love and serve the Lord, rejoicing in the power of the Holy Spirit.

THE BLESSING

God the Father, God the Son, and God the Holy Spirit, bless, preserve and keep you, now and always. Amen.

228